Standards for Blood Banks and Transfusion Services

26th Edition

AABB
8101 Glenbrook Road
Bethesda, Maryland 20814-2749
United States of America

ISBN 978-1-56395-289-0
Printed in the United States

THE AABB STANDARDS PROGRAM COMMITTEE

Committee Members
Harvey G. Klein, MD, Chair
Michael L. Baird, PhD
Sarah J. Ilstrup, MD
Steven Kleinman, MD
German F. Leparc, BS, MD
Dawn Michelle, MT(ASCP)SBB
Tania Motschman, MS, MT(ASCP)SBB, CQA(ASQ)
Joann M. Moulds, PhD, MT(ASCP)SBB
Doug Padley, MT(ASCP)
Thomas H. Price, MD

Liaisons Representing Other AABB Committees
Accreditation Program Committee–Kathleen Sazama, MD, JD
Education Program Committee–Kaaron Benson, MD

Representatives from Other Organizations
Armed Services Blood Program Office (DoD)–Lt. Col. Michael Lopatka, MS, MT(ASCP)SBB
American Society of Hematology–Leslie Silberstein, MD
Food and Drug Administration–Judy E. Ciaraldi, BS, MT(ASCP)SBB, CQA(ASQ);
    Helen Cowley, MT(ASCP)SBB, CQA(ASQ); David Keith
Héma-Québec–Gilles Delage, MD

QUALITY MANAGEMENT SUBCOMMITTEE

Committee Members
Tania Motschman, MS, MT(ASCP)SBB, CQA(ASQ), Chair
Joanne Lynn Becker, MD
Rosalie Dvorak-Remis, MHS, MT(ASCP)SBB
Betsy W. Jett, MT(ASCP), CQA(ASQ)CQMgr
Regina M. Leger, MSQA, MT(ASCP)SBB, CQMgr(ASQ)
Patrick W. Ooley, MS, MT(ASCP), CQA(ASQ)
Jane Pritchard, BS, MT(ASCP), CLSp(MB)

Liaison Representing Other AABB Committee
Accreditation Program Committee–Leane Ziebell, MSA, MT(ASCP)SBB, CQA(ASQ)

Consultant
Lucia M. Berte, MA, MT(ASCP)SBB, DLM, CQA(ASQ)CMQ/OE

PREFACE

The Standards Program Committee (SPC) is an umbrella committee whose primary role is to oversee the creation, development, and revision of all AABB standards to ensure harmonization and consistency in AABB standard-setting activities. The SPC consists of a committee chair, the chair of the Quality Management Subcommittee (QMS), the chair of the Standards Subcommittee for the Evaluation of International Variances, as well as the chairs of the five specialty program units.

The QMS develops and reviews quality standards and guidance to ensure that all quality management concepts incorporate a consistent message. The program units are responsible for creating the technical standards based on a review of current scientific and medical data, when available. Program units are also responsible for creating guidance documents that clarify the intent of standards and that include recommendations on how to implement technical requirements.

The Blood Bank/Transfusion Service (BB/TS) Standards Program Unit (SPU) developed this 26th edition of *Standards for Blood Banks and Transfusion Services (BB/TS Standards)*. The BB/TS SPU used an evidence-based decision making process, when possible, to modify existing requirements or create new specific requirements. These *BB/TS Standards* are based on input from a variety of sources, including comments from AABB members, public members on the program unit, and recognized experts in blood banking and transfusion medicine. With this edition, the quality management system remains the framework of the publication, resulting in the 10 chapter headings representing the 10 Quality System Essentials, which were first identified in AABB Association Bulletin #97-4.

Under this structure, the most general quality standards appear at the beginning of each chapter. These general standards require that the blood bank or transfusion service have policies, processes, and procedures to meet the intent of the chapter. The standards that follow are more specific and usually require the existence of policies, processes, and procedures that address elements of a facility's day-to-day operations. The most specific requirements are reference standards, which are presented as charts. Reference standards contain information that is most easily summarized and understood when presented as charts. It is important to note, however, that all requirements are of equal importance, whether contained in a chart, a specific technical requirement, or a general quality standard. A requirement, once stated, is not repeated because it applies throughout all of the *BB/TS Standards*.

When a pen symbol (✐) precedes a standard, a record requirement is associated with the fulfillment of the standard. The reader should refer to Reference Standards 6.2A through 6.2E at the end of Chapter 6, Documents and Records, for the specific record to be maintained and the associated retention time. In an effort to avoid redundancy, the record creation requirements in Reference Standards 6.2A through 6.2E are linked to standards that concern activities in the remainder of the document. In some cases, the reference standards may address specific tasks in greater detail than the corresponding standard.

As in the past, references to regulatory resources are provided for informational purposes to highlight where federal regulations or guidelines differ or expand on the requirements set forth by AABB. The BB/TS SPU's intent is that, unless a standard specifically states that the cited documents and regulations apply, citations of regulatory documents do not inherently require the facility to comply with the referenced document. In a few instances, the BB/TS SPU referenced draft Food and Drug Administration documents because it determined that they reflect the standard of care.

Because blood centers and transfusion services may store and provide tissue or derivatives in conjunction with blood and components, these products are included in the general quality standards and in the storage and transportation standards, but are otherwise minimally addressed throughout the *BB/TS Standards*. However, it is not the intent of the BB/TS SPU to require that storage and release of these products be the responsibility of the blood bank or transfusion service. In instances where these activities are beyond the scope of the user, the requirements do not apply. All record requirements that pertain to tissues and derivatives can be reviewed in Reference Standards 6.2D and 6.2E. Efforts have been made to conform record retention requirements for tissue-related activities with those set forth by the American Association of Tissue Banks.

Although there are unique requirements for tissue or derivatives, there are many other standards in this document that apply to them as well. General quality concepts (including traceability, inspection, and testing; validation of storage and transportation methods; appropriate storage conditions; and other such requirements) apply to any products that a blood bank or transfusion service may collect, process, ship for further processing, or release for administration. Although collection facilities cannot always control the source of tissue and derivatives, all plasma for manufacture is required to be collected from donors that have been qualified and accepted in conformance with the *BB/TS Standards*. Any activities or products addressed in the *BB/TS Standards* should be included under the rubric of the facility's quality management system.

Significant changes from the 25th edition of *BB/TS Standards* are detailed on the AABB Web site, www.aabb.org.

I would like to express my personal thanks to the participants in the BB/TS SPU, all of whom contributed their time, expertise, and common sense to the development of the 26th edition. Special thanks go to the work group chairs—Debbie Kessler, Tom Carson, and Pat Ooley for their outstanding efforts and additional time commitments. Finally, many thanks are due to Eduardo Nunes and Christopher Bocquet at the AABB National Office for their support, guidance, expertise, dedication, patience, and sense of humor.

Thomas H. Price, MD
Chair, Blood Bank/Transfusion Service Standards Program Unit

INTRODUCTION

T he *Standards for Blood Banks and Transfusion Services (BB/TS Standards)* was prepared by the Blood Bank/Transfusion Services Standards Program Unit (BB/TS SPU), the Quality Management Subcommittee, and the Standards Program Committee of AABB. The goal of the *BB/TS Standards* is to maintain and enhance the quality and safety of transfusion and transplantation, and to provide a basis for the AABB Accreditation Program. The effective date of this 26th edition of *BB/TS Standards*, for the purposes of AABB activities, is November 1, 2009.

For the purposes of this publication, a blood bank collects, stores, processes, and transports human blood intended for transfusion; a transfusion service issues blood and blood components for transfusion. Although these services are typically performed as described, some services may be performed in either a blood bank or a transfusion service. A blood bank or transfusion service may, in addition, store and provide tissue. The blood bank or transfusion service can at times maintain and dispense derivatives as well. Requirements for each of these activities are described in this document.

Notes on Language

Some terms or phrases are specifically defined for purposes of these *BB/TS Standards*. The term "shall" is used to indicate a mandatory statement and describe the single acceptable activity or method; failure to meet the specified requirement would constitute a nonconformance under the AABB Accreditation Program. The phrase "the blood bank or transfusion service shall have a policy" or "have a process" indicates that the institution must have a specific policy or process to achieve the goal required by the standard. The word "should" is used to indicate a recommendation. "Should" is advisory, but is not required for accreditation. It indicates a commonly accepted activity for which there may be effective alternatives.

The term "may" is used to reflect an acceptable method or practice that is recognized but not required. The phrase "by a method known to" refers to published data can be used to demonstrate the acceptability of a process or procedure. The term "specified requirements" refers to requirements derived from, standards, federal regulations, customer agreements, practice standards, requirements of an accrediting organization, or other sources.

A glossary is included for the purpose of defining terms to reflect their usage in the context of these *BB/TS Standards*, not general usage. Therefore, it is recommended that users of these *BB/TS Standards* review the glossary before reviewing the standards. Readers will also find a list of common abbreviations used throughout the *BB/TS Standards* inside the back cover.

Notes on Format

BB/TS Standards represents accepted performance requirements that may be exceeded in practice. Many organizations working in special situations can, and should, be more rigorous in their internal requirements. *BB/TS Standards* has been developed on the basis of good medical practice and, when available, scientific data. There may be legal requirements of federal, state, and local governments that apply as well. Although the majority of the standards are in compliance with applicable federal laws and requirements, no assurances can be given that compliance with *BB/TS Standards* will result in compliance with all applicable laws and requirements. The *BB/TS Standards* is not intended as a substitute for legal advice and the content should not be relied upon for legal purposes. Blood banks and transfusion services must make their own determinations as to how best to ensure compliance with all applicable laws and requirements—whether federal, state, or local—including, if necessary, consulting with legal counsel familiar with these issues.

Every effort was made to take all existing technologies into account; however, in some areas, the manufacturer's directions for the use of a device or the requirements for its use may be more proscriptive or even in conflict with the requirements contained in this publication. In these cases, the device or material should be used in accordance with the manufacturer's directions. Users of this publication who encounter such issues are encouraged to submit their feedback to the Standards Development Department (standards@aabb.org) at the AABB National Office.

Regulatory and Legal Issues, AABB Variances, and Other Considerations

Alternative methods or approaches that deviate from the *BB/TS Standards* may, at times, allow equally safe practice. Such situations are infrequent, and for accredited organizations, alternative methods cannot be used to meet requirements of *BB/TS Standards* without prior express written approval of the BB/TS SPU. Thus, for accreditation purposes, the written policy, process, or procedure and the approval of the variance from the Standards Program Unit must be available in the blood bank or transfusion service. At the beginning of each new standards revision cycle, approved variances will be considered and may result in revision of the standard. With each new edition of *BB/TS Standards*, the institution may reapply for the variance.

Variance requests must be submitted to the BB/TS SPU, care of the AABB National Office. Request forms can be found on the AABB Web site (www.aabb.org) by clicking on Members Area>Standards (http://www. aabb.org/Content/Members_Area/Standards/standards.htm). When a variance is granted, some information about the variance is made available to the public, including the name of the facility, a brief description of variance, and the date on which the variance expires. Variances are valid for one edition of *Standards.* If variances are denied, requestors may appeal unfavorable outcomes to a Standards Review Committee.

Investigative studies may necessitate deviation from the *BB/TS Standards*. Such studies must 1) be performed under the direction of qualified individuals with consideration for the therapeutic requirements of the patient and the safety of the patient and donor, and 2) avoid supplanting or eliminating the requirements of these *BB/TS Standards* whenever possible. Scientific studies that modify or replace these requirements must be approved by the Institutional Review Board Committee on Experimentation on Human Subjects or the equivalent peer-review group. The approval must be available in the blood bank or transfusion service.

These *BB/TS Standards* may not necessarily apply to policies, processes, or procedures involving the Department of Defense or its military services during contingency operations. In addition, urgent medical conditions may warrant abbreviation of practices required by the *BB/TS Standards*; a record of the need to do so must be maintained.

Although the *BB/TS Standards* do provide a great amount of technical information concerning the blood banking community, other AABB publications provide more specific recommendations. When using this edition of the *BB/TS Standards*, having access to the current edition of the AABB *Technical Manual*, and the current edition of the *Circular of Information for the Use of Human Blood and Blood Components* could be of service in understanding and implementing these requirements. Guidance for specific standards that appear in this edition of the *BB/TS Standards* will be published in *Standards Source*, available online at the AABB Web site. *Standards Source* entries are crafted from member clarification requests and approved variances. All requests for clarification of a standard should be sent to the AABB Standards Development Department via e-mail (standards@aabb.org) or by fax at 301.907.6895.

The guiding principle of this document is to be consistent with available scientific information while focusing on patient advocacy and optimal care for donors who provide blood and components. The requirements are intended to be simple, clear, and practical. The use of the *BB/TS Standards* should aid materially in developing and maintaining policies, processes, and procedures that will provide safe and effective transfusion and transplantation, as well as a safe work environment for blood bank and transfusion service personnel.

TABLE OF CONTENTS

Table of Contents

Table of Contents

1. ORGANIZATION

1.0 Organization
The blood bank or transfusion service shall have a structure that clearly defines and documents the parties responsible for the provision of blood, components, tissue, derivatives, and services and the relationship of individuals responsible for key quality functions.

1.1 Executive Management
The blood bank or transfusion service shall have a defined executive management. Executive management shall have:
1) Responsibility and authority for the blood bank's or transfusion service's operations.
2) The authority to establish or make changes to the blood bank's or transfusion service's quality system.
3) The responsibility for compliance with these *BB/TS Standards* and applicable laws and regulations.
4) Participation in management review of the quality system.

1.1.1 Medical Director Responsibilities
The blood bank or transfusion service shall have a medical director who is a licensed physician and qualified by education, training, and/or experience. The medical director shall have responsibility and authority for all medical and technical policies, processes, and procedures—including those that pertain to laboratory personnel and test performance—and for the consultative and support services that relate to the care and safety of donors and/or transfusion recipients. The medical director may delegate these responsibilities to another qualified physician; however, the medical director shall retain ultimate responsibility for medical director duties.

1.2 Quality System
A quality system shall be defined, documented, implemented, and maintained. All personnel shall be trained in its application.

1.2.1 Quality Representative
The quality system shall be under the supervision of a designated person who reports to executive management.

1.2.2   Management Reviews
Management shall assess the effectiveness of the quality system through scheduled management reviews.

1.3   Policies, Processes, and Procedures
Quality and operational policies, processes, and procedures shall be developed and implemented to ensure that the requirements of these *BB/TS Standards* are satisfied. All such policies, processes, and procedures shall be in writing or captured electronically and shall be followed. Standard 5.1.1 applies.

1.3.1   The medical director shall approve all medical and technical policies, processes, and procedures.

1.3.2   Any exceptions to policies, processes, and procedures warranted by clinical situations shall require justification and preapproval by the medical director on a case-by-case basis.

1.4   Emergency Preparedness
The blood bank or transfusion service shall have emergency operation policies, processes, and procedures to respond to the effects of internal and external disasters.

1.5   Communication of Concerns
The blood bank or transfusion service shall have a process for personnel to anonymously communicate concerns about quality or safety to executive management and/or to AABB. Standard 9.1 applies.

2. RESOURCES

2.0 Resources
The blood bank or transfusion service shall have policies, processes, and procedures that ensure the provision of adequate resources to perform, verify, and manage all activities in the blood bank or transfusion service.

2.1 Human Resources
The blood bank or transfusion service shall have a process to ensure the employment of an adequate number of individuals qualified by education, training, and/or experience. Current job descriptions shall be maintained and shall define appropriate qualifications for each job position.

2.1.1 Qualification
Personnel performing critical tasks shall be qualified to perform assigned activities on the basis of appropriate education, training, and/or experience.

2.1.2 Training
The blood bank or transfusion service shall have a process for identifying training needs and shall provide training for personnel performing critical tasks.

2.1.3 Competence
Evaluations of competence shall be performed before independent performance of assigned activities and at specified intervals.[*]

2.1.4 Personnel Records
Personnel records for each employee shall be maintained.

2.1.4.1 For those authorized to perform or review critical tasks, records of names, signatures, initials or identification codes, and inclusive dates of employment shall be maintained.

---

[*]42 CFR 493.1235 and 42 CFR 493.1451(b)(8)(9).

3. EQUIPMENT

3.0 Equipment

The blood bank or transfusion service shall identify the equipment that is critical to the provision of blood, components, tissue, derivatives, and/or services. The blood bank or transfusion service shall have policies, processes, and procedures to ensure that calibration, maintenance, and monitoring of equipment conform to these *BB/TS Standards* and other specified requirements.

3.1 Selection of Equipment

The blood bank or transfusion service shall have a process to define the selection criteria for equipment.

3.2 Qualification of Equipment

All equipment shall be qualified for its intended use, including Food and Drug Administration (FDA)-cleared or approved devices.

3.3 Use of Equipment

Equipment shall be used in accordance with the manufacturer's written instructions.

3.4 Unique Identification of Equipment

Equipment shall have unique identification. Standard 5.1.6.2 applies.

3.5 Equipment Monitoring and Maintenance

The blood bank or transfusion service shall have a process for scheduled monitoring and maintenance of equipment that at a minimum is in accordance with manufacturer's instructions. The process shall include: frequency of checks, check methods, acceptance criteria, and actions to be taken for unsatisfactory results.

3.5.1 Calibration of Equipment

Calibrations and/or adjustments shall be performed using equipment and materials that have adequate accuracy and precision. At a minimum, calibrations and/or adjustments shall be performed:
1) Before use.
2) After activities that may affect the calibration.
3) At prescribed intervals.

4

3.5.1.1   There shall be safeguards to prevent equipment from adjustments that would invalidate the calibrated setting. Standard 5.1.3 applies.

3.5.2   Investigation and Follow-up

Investigation and follow-up of equipment malfunctions, failures, or adverse events shall include:
1) Assessment of blood, components, tissue, derivatives, and services provided when equipment is found to be out of calibration.
2) Assessment of the effect on donor eligibility and donor and patient safety.
3) Steps to ensure that the equipment is removed from service.
4) Investigation of the malfunction, failure, or adverse event.
5) Steps for requalification of the equipment.
6) Reporting the nature of the malfunction, failure, or adverse event to the manufacturer, when indicated.

Chapter 7, Deviations, Nonconformances, and Adverse Events, applies.

3.6   Storage Devices for Blood, Components, Reagents, Tissue, and Derivatives

3.6.1   Storage devices shall have the capacity and design to ensure that the proper temperature is maintained. Standard 5.1.8.1.2 applies.

3.6.2   Refrigerators, freezers, and platelet incubators shall have their temperature monitored.

3.6.3   If storage utilizes liquid nitrogen, either liquid nitrogen levels or temperature shall be monitored.

3.7   Alarm Systems

Storage devices for blood, components, tissue and derivatives shall have alarms and shall conform to the following standards (Standard 5.1.3 applies):

3.7.1   The alarm shall be set to activate under conditions that will allow proper action to be taken before blood, components, tissue, or derivatives reach unacceptable conditions.

3.7.2   The alarm system in liquid nitrogen freezers shall be activated before the contained liquid nitrogen reaches an unacceptable level.

3.7.3   Activation of the alarm shall initiate a process for immediate investigation and appropriate corrective action.

3.8 Warming Devices for Blood and Components

Warming devices shall be equipped with a temperature-sensing device and a warning system to detect malfunctions and prevent hemolysis or other damage to blood or components.

3.9 Computer Systems

The blood bank or transfusion service shall have processes to support the implementation and modification of software, hardware, and databases relating to the requirements of these *BB/TS Standards*. Standard 5.1.1 applies. These processes shall include:

1) Risk analysis, training, validation, implementation, and evaluation of postimplementation performance.
2) System maintenance and operation.
3) Documentation written in language understandable to the user.
4) Display and verification of data before final acceptance, when data are added, or when data are amended.
5) Evaluation, authorization, and documentation of modifications to the system

3.9.1 Computer System Records

Records of the following shall be maintained:

1) Validation of system software, hardware, databases, user-defined tables, electronic data transfer, and/or electronic data receipt.
2) Fulfillment of applicable life-cycle requirements for internally developed software.*
3) Numerical designation of system versions, if applicable, with inclusive dates of use.
4) Monitoring of data integrity for critical data elements.

3.9.2

An alternative system that ensures continuous operation shall be available in the event that computerized data and computer-assisted functions are unavailable. The alternative system shall be tested periodically. Processes and procedures shall address mitigation of the effects of disasters and recovery plans.

---

*21 CFR 820.30.

FDA Guidance for Industry, January 11, 2002, "General Principles of Software Validation; Final Guidance for Industry and FDA Staff."

FDA Guidance, May 11, 2005, "Guidance for the Content of Premarket Submissions for Software Contained in Medical Devices."

3.9.3 Personnel responsible for management of computer systems shall be responsible for compliance with the regulations that affect their use.

3.9.4 There shall be processes and procedures to support the management of computer systems.

3.9.5 A system designed to prevent unauthorized access to computers and electronic records shall be established and followed.

4. SUPPLIER AND CUSTOMER ISSUES

4.0 Supplier and Customer Issues
The blood bank or transfusion service shall have policies, processes, and procedures to evaluate the ability of suppliers of critical materials, equipment, and services to consistently meet specified requirements.

4.1 Supplier Qualification
The blood bank or transfusion service shall evaluate and participate in the selection of suppliers, when possible, before acceptance of an agreement.

4.1.1 When a supplier fails to meet specified requirements, it shall be reported to the management with contracting authority.

4.1.2 Testing or services required by these *BB/TS Standards* shall be performed in a laboratory accredited by AABB or an equivalent accrediting body.

4.1.2.1 Laboratory testing shall be performed in a laboratory certified by the Centers for Medicare and Medicaid Services (CMS) and registered with the FDA, if indicated by 21 CFR 610.40(f).

4.2 Agreements
Agreements, or changes to agreements, shall define supplier and customer expectations and shall reflect agreement.

4.2.1 Agreement Review
Agreements and any incorporated changes shall be reviewed and communicated.

4.2.2 The responsibilities for activities covered by these *BB/TS Standards* when more than one facility is involved shall be specified by agreement.

4.3 Incoming Receipt, Inspection, and Testing
Incoming blood, components, tissue, derivatives, and critical materials shall be received, inspected, and tested, as necessary, before acceptance or use.

4.3.1   Each container used for collection, preservation, and storage shall be inspected to ensure that it is intact. The label shall be complete, affixed, and legible. Reference Standard 5.1.6A, Requirements for Labeling Blood and Components, applies.

4.3.2   Critical materials shall meet specified requirements.

4.3.2.1   All containers and solutions used for collection, preservation, and storage and all reagents used for required tests on blood samples shall meet or exceed applicable FDA criteria.

5. PROCESS CONTROL

5.0 Process Control

The blood bank or transfusion service shall have policies and validated processes and procedures that ensure the quality of the blood, components, tissue, derivatives, and services. The blood bank or transfusion service shall ensure that these policies, processes, and procedures are carried out under controlled conditions.

5.1 General Elements

5.1.1 Change Control

The blood bank or transfusion service shall have a process to develop new processes and procedures or change existing ones. This process shall include identification of specifications and verification that specifications have been met. Before implementation, the new or changed processes and procedures shall be validated. Standard 2.1.2 applies.

5.1.2 Proficiency Testing Program

The blood bank or transfusion service shall participate in a proficiency testing program, if available, for testing regulated by the Clinical Laboratory Improvement Amendments and performed by the facility.* When a CMS-approved program is not available, there shall be a system for determining the accuracy and reliability of test results. Results shall be reviewed and corrective action taken, where appropriate, when expected results are not achieved.

5.1.3 Quality Control

A program of quality control shall be established that is sufficiently comprehensive to ensure that reagents, equipment, and methods function as expected. Chapter 9, Process Improvement Through Corrective and Preventive Action, applies.

5.1.4 Use of Materials

All materials (including containers and solutions used for collection, preservation, and storage of blood, blood components, and all reagents used for required tests on blood samples) shall be stored and used in accordance with the manufacturer's written instructions and shall meet specified requirements. Standard 3.6 applies.

---

*42 CFR 493.1236.

5.1.4.1   Reagents that are prepared by the facility shall meet or exceed applicable FDA criteria.*

5.1.5   Sterility
Aseptic methods shall be employed to minimize the risk of microbial contamination of blood and blood components. Equipment and solutions that come into direct contact with blood or components shall be sterile and pyrogen-free. Single-use equipment shall be used whenever possible.

5.1.5.1   The blood bank or transfusion service shall have methods to limit and to detect or inactivate bacteria in all platelet components. Standard 5.6.2 applies.

5.1.5.2   When a true culture-positive result is obtained and an appropriate specimen is available, additional testing to identify the organism shall be performed. Additional testing and follow-up shall be defined. Standards 5.2.3 and 7.1 to 7.1.4 apply.

5.1.6   Identification and Traceability

5.1.6.1   Process or Procedure Steps
For each critical step in collection, processing, compatibility testing, and transportation of blood components, tissue, and derivatives there shall be a mechanism to identify who performed the step and when it was performed.

5.1.6.2   Traceability
The blood bank or transfusion service shall ensure that all blood, components, tissue, derivatives, and critical materials used in their processing, as well as laboratory samples and donor and patient records, are identified and traceable.

5.1.6.3   General Labeling Requirements
The blood bank or transfusion service shall have a labeling process. This process shall include all steps taken to: 1) identify the original unit, any components, and any compo-

---

*FDA Draft Guideline, March 1992, "Recommended Methods for Blood Grouping Reagents Evaluation." [Docket No.84S-0181]
21 CFR 660.20 to 660.28.

nent modifications; 2) complete the required reviews; and 3) attach the appropriate labels. Standard 5.9.1 applies.

5.1.6.3.1   The following requirements shall apply:
1) Labeling of blood and component containers shall be in conformance with the most recent version of the United States Industry Consensus Standard for the Uniform Labeling of Blood and Blood Components using ISBT 128.[*] Units conforming to 1985 FDA Uniform Labeling Guidelines are acceptable if collected and labeled before May 1, 2008.[†]
2) The original label and added portions of the label shall be attached to the container and shall be in clear, eye-readable type. Additionally, the ABO/Rh, donation identification number, product code, and facility identification shall be in machine-readable format.[‡] The label shall include the applicable items required in Reference Standard 5.1.6A, Requirements for Labeling Blood and Components.
3) Handwritten additions or changes shall be legible and applied with permanent, moisture-proof ink.
4) All modifications to component labels shall be specified and controlled.
5) If a component is modified and new labels are applied, the labeling process shall include a method to ensure the accuracy of all labels including the donation identification number, ABO/Rh, expiration date (as appropriate), and product name and code.
6) The labeling process shall include a second check to ensure the accuracy of affixed label(s) including the correct donation identification number, ABO/Rh, expiration date (as appropriate), and product name and code.

---

[*]FDA Guidance, September 22, 2006, "Industry Consensus Standard for the Uniform Labeling of Blood and Blood Components Using ISBT 128 version 2.0, November 2005."
[†]Units collected and labeled before ISBT 128 implementation may be relabeled using Codabar.
[‡]21 CFR 606.121(c)(13).

5.1.6.4 Donor Identification

Blood collection facilities shall confirm donor identity and link the repeat donor to existing donor records.

5.1.6.5 Unit Identification

The labeling system shall make it possible to trace any unit of blood, blood component (including those in a pool), or tissue from source to final disposition. The system shall allow recheck of records applying to the specific unit or tissue, including investigation of reported adverse events.

5.1.6.5.1
A unique identification shall be affixed by the collecting or pooling facility to each unit of blood, component, and attached containers, or a tissue specimen or lot. This identification shall not be obscured, altered, or removed by facilities that subsequently handle the unit.

5.1.6.5.2
If a transfusing facility or other intermediate shipping facility receives a unit labeled with a Codabar Donation Identification Number, an ISBT 128 Donation Identification or Codabar Donation Identification Number may be assigned. The label shall be affixed to the container and shall identify the facility assigning the identification. Any other donation identification number, except that of the original collecting facility shall be removed, obscured, or obliterated. This requirement does not preclude the use of a patient identification number.

5.1.6.5.3
No more than two donation identifications shall be visible on a blood or product container, one of which shall be that of the original collecting facility. This requirement does not preclude the use of a patient identification number.

5.1.7 Inspection

The blood bank or transfusion service shall have a process to ensure that blood, components, and services are inspected at facility-defined stages to verify that specified requirements are met. For tissue and derivatives, Standard 4.3 applies.

5.1.8 Handling, Storage, and Transportation

The blood bank or transfusion service shall have a process to ensure that blood, components, tissue, derivatives, samples, and critical materials (including reagents) are handled, stored, and transported in a manner that prevents damage, limits deterioration, and meets requirements contained in Reference Standard 5.1.8A, Requirements for Storage, Transportation, and Expiration.

5.1.8.1 Storage Conditions

5.1.8.1.1 The blood bank or transfusion service shall ensure the appropriate segregation of blood and components, including autologous units.

5.1.8.1.2 For storage of blood products, the temperature shall be continuously monitored or the temperature shall be recorded at least every 4 hours.

5.1.8.1.2.1 If blood or components are stored in an open storage area, the ambient temperature shall be recorded at least every 4 hours.

5.1.8.1.3 Tissue shall be stored in accordance with the manufacturer's instructions.

5.1.8.1.4 Access to storage areas and authorization to remove contents shall be controlled.

5.1.8.2 Transportation

Blood, components, tissue, and derivatives shall be inspected immediately before packing for shipment and shipped for transfusion or transplantation only if specified requirements are met.

5.1.8.2.1 Containers (eg, portable coolers) used to transport blood components issued for transfusion shall be qualified and the process validated for the appropriate transport temperature.

Collection and Production of Components

5.2 Information, Consents, and Notifications

5.2.1 Donor Education

The blood bank shall have procedures to ensure that the following requirements are met for all prospective donors:

1) Donors are given educational materials regarding infectious diseases transmitted by blood transfusion.

2) Donors are informed of the signs and symptoms of AIDS.*

3) Donors acknowledge that the educational materials have been read.

4) Donors are informed of the importance of providing accurate information.

5) Donors are informed of the importance of withdrawing themselves from the donation process if they believe that their blood is not suitable for transfusion.

5.2.2

When parental permission is required, the collection facility shall have a process to provide information concerning the donation process to parents or the legally authorized representative of the donor.

5.2.3 Donor Consent

The consent of all donors shall be obtained before donation. Elements of the donation procedure shall be explained to the prospective donor in understandable terms. The explanation shall include information about risks of the procedure and tests performed to reduce the risks of transmission of infectious diseases to the allogeneic recipient. The donor shall have an opportunity to ask questions and have them answered and to give or refuse consent for donation. In the case of a minor or a legally incompetent adult, consent shall be addressed in accordance with applicable law.

5.2.3.1

A prospective donor shall be informed that there are circumstances in which infectious disease tests are not performed.

---

*FDA Memorandum, April 23, 1992, "Revised Recommendation for the Prevention of Human Immunodeficiency Virus (HIV) Transmission by Blood and Blood Products."

5.2.3.2   Confidential Unit Exclusion
If an opportunity is provided to the donor at the time of donation to indicate that blood collected should not be used for transfusion, the donor shall be informed that the blood will be subjected to testing and that there will be notification of any positive infectious disease test results. Standard 5.2.3.1 applies.

5.2.4   Donor Notification of Abnormal Findings and Test Results
The medical director shall establish the means to notify all donors (including autologous donors) of any medically significant abnormality detected during the predonation evaluation or as a result of laboratory testing or recipient follow-up. In the case of autologous donors, the referring physician shall also be notified. Appropriate education, counseling, and referral shall be offered.* Standard 5.8.5.1 applies.

5.3   Care of Donors

5.3.1   The collection facility shall have a policy to ensure that the donor qualification process is private and confidential.

5.3.2   The donor shall be observed during the donation and for a length of time thereafter, as defined by the facility's policies and procedures.

5.3.2.1   The collection facility shall have a process for treating donor adverse events and providing for emergency medical care as necessary. Immediate assistance and the necessary equipment and supplies shall be available. Standard 7.3 applies.

5.3.3   Postphlebotomy Advice
The donor shall be instructed in postphlebotomy care.

5.4   Donor Qualification

5.4.1   Allogeneic Donor Qualification
The prospective donor shall meet the donor qualification requirements contained in Reference Standard 5.4.1A, Requirements for Allogeneic Donor Qualification.

---

*21 CFR 630.6.

5.4.1.1 The collection facility shall ensure that donor red cell losses for all donations and samples collected during any rolling 12-month period do not exceed the loss of red cells permitted for whole blood collections.*

5.4.1.2 Postdonation Information About Donors
The collection facility shall have a process for managing postdonation information received from the donor or a third party about a donor's eligibility.

5.4.2 Protection of the Recipient
On the day of donation and before collection, the prospective donor's history shall be evaluated and the donor examined to exclude donation by a person with evidence of disease transmissible by blood transfusion or other conditions thought to compromise the suitability of the blood or component. Reference Standard 5.4.1A, Requirements for Allogeneic Donor Qualification, applies.

5.4.2.1 Donors implicated in a transfusion-related acute lung injury (TRALI) event or associated with multiple events of TRALI shall be evaluated regarding their continued eligibility to donate.

5.4.3 Protection of the Donor
On the day of donation and before collection, the prospective donor's history shall be evaluated and the donor examined to minimize the risk of harm to the donor.

5.4.4 Autologous Donor Qualification
Because of the special circumstances related to autologous blood transfusion, rigid criteria for donor selection are not required. In situations where requirements for allogeneic donor selection or collection are not applied, alternate requirements shall be defined and documented by the medical director. Standard 1.3.2 applies. Autologous donor qualification requirements shall include:

---

*FDA Memorandum, December 4, 1995, "Donor Deferral Due to Red Cell Loss During Collection of Source Plasma by Automated Plasmapheresis."

FDA Guidance for Industry, February 13, 2001, "Technical Correction: Recommendations for Collecting Red Blood Cells by Automated Apheresis Methods."

FDA Guidance for Industry and FDA Review Staff, December 17, 2007, "Collection of Platelets by Automated Methods."

5.4.4.1   A medical order from the patient's physician is required to collect blood for autologous use.

5.4.4.2   The hemoglobin concentration of the autologous donor's blood shall be ≥11 g/dL or the hematocrit, if used, shall be ≥33%. Blood obtained by earlobe puncture shall not be used for this determination.

5.4.4.3   All blood collections from the autologous donor shall be completed more than 72 hours before the time of anticipated surgery or transfusion.

5.4.4.4   An autologous donor shall be deferred when he or she has a clinical condition for which there is a risk of bacteremia.

5.4.4.5   The unit shall be reserved for autologous transfusion.

5.5   Additional Apheresis Donor Qualification Requirements

5.5.1   Selection of Donors

With the exception of the donation interval, the standards that apply to allogeneic donor qualification shall apply to the selection of apheresis donors. Donors who do not meet allogeneic donor requirements shall undergo apheresis only when the components are expected to be of particular value to an intended recipient and only when approved by the medical director.

5.5.2   Automated Plasmapheresis Donation

5.5.2.1   Infrequent Plasmapheresis Program

In an "infrequent" plasmapheresis program, donors shall undergo plasmapheresis no more frequently than once every 4 weeks. The plasmapheresis donor shall weigh at least 50 kg (110 lb).[*]

---

[*]FDA Memorandum, March 10, 1995, "Revision of FDA Memorandum of August 27, 1982: Requirements for Infrequent Plasmapheresis Donors."

5.5.2.2   Frequent Plasmapheresis Program

In a "frequent" plasmapheresis program, in which plasma is donated more frequently than once every 4 weeks, the FDA requirements for donor testing and evaluation by a physical exam shall be followed.[*]

5.5.2.2.1   Collection shall occur a maximum of two times in a 7-day period and the interval be-tween two collections shall be at least 2 days.[†]

5.5.3   Automated Cytapheresis Donations

5.5.3.1   The interval between procedures for platelet, granulocyte, and leukocyte donors shall be at least 2 days and the total volume of plasma collected shall not exceed the volume of plasma cleared by the FDA for the instrument. A donor shall undergo the procedure a maximum of two times in a 7-day period, not to exceed 24 times in a rolling 12 months, except in unusual circumstances as determined by the blood bank medical director. Standard 5.4.1.1 applies.[‡]

5.5.3.2   If a platelet, granulocyte, or leukocyte donor donates a unit of Whole Blood, at least 8 weeks shall elapse before a subsequent automated cytapheresis procedure, unless the extracorporeal red cell volume of the apheresis machine does not exceed 100 mL. Standards 5.4.1.1 and 5.5.3.1 apply.

5.5.3.3   If it becomes impossible to return the donor's red cells during apheresis, at least 8 weeks shall elapse before a subsequent apheresis procedure, unless the red cell loss was <200 mL. Standards 5.4.1.1 and 5.5.3.1 apply.[§]

---

[*]21 CFR 640.65.

[†]FDA Memorandum, November 4, 1992, "Volume Limits for Automated Collection of Source Plasma."

[‡]FDA Guidance for Industry and FDA Review Staff, December 17, 2007, "Collection of Platelets by Automated Methods."

[§]FDA Guidance for Industry, February 13, 2001, "Technical Correction: Recommendations for Collecting Red Blood Cells by Automated Apheresis Methods."

5.5.3.4 **Plateletpheresis Donors**
A blood sample shall be collected before each procedure for the determination of the donor's platelet count. If the result is available, it shall be used as the platelet count to qualify the donor.

5.5.3.4.1 If the result of the predonation platelet count is not available, the donor's most recent platelet count may be used to qualify the donor. Triple collections of Apheresis Platelets may not be collected from first-time donors unless a qualifying platelet count is obtained from a sample collected before donation.

5.5.3.4.2 The results of platelet counts performed before or after a procedure may be used to qualify the donor for the next procedure.

5.5.3.4.3 Plateletpheresis donors whose counts are <150,000/μL shall be deferred from plateletpheresis donation until a subsequent platelet count is at least 150,000/μL.[*]

5.5.3.5 **2-Unit Red Cell Apheresis Donors**
The donor of a 2-unit red cell apheresis collection shall meet specific hemoglobin/hematocrit and weight requirements for the device cleared by the FDA.[†]

5.5.3.5.1 The donor shall be deferred for 16 weeks following a 2-unit red cell apheresis collection.

5.5.3.5.2 **2-Unit Red Cell Collection**
The volume of red cells removed from apheresis donors shall not exceed a volume predicted to result in a donor hematocrit of <30% or a hemoglobin <10 g/dL after volume replacement.

---

[*]FDA Guidance for Industry and FDA Review Staff, December 17, 2007, "Collection of Platelets by Automated Methods."

[†]FDA Guidance for Industry, February 13, 2001, "Technical Correction: Recommendations for Collecting Red Blood Cells by Automated Apheresis Methods."

5.5.4   Multiple Concurrent Apheresis Collection

The donor eligibility criteria and interval between donations shall meet FDA criteria. The combined volume limits of red cells and plasma removed from the donor shall follow criteria for the FDA-cleared device used.*

5.6   Blood Collection

5.6.1   Methods

Blood shall be collected into a sterile closed system.

5.6.2   Protection Against Contamination

The venipuncture site shall be prepared so as to minimize risk of bacterial contamination. Green soap (USP) shall not be used.

5.6.2.1   Blood collection containers with draw line (inlet) diversion pouches shall be used for any collection of platelets, including whole blood from which platelets are made.

5.6.3   Samples for Laboratory Tests

5.6.3.1   At the time of collection or component preparation, the integral donor tubing shall be filled with anticoagulated blood and sealed in such a manner that it will be available for subsequent compatibility testing.

5.6.3.1.1   The integral donor tubing segments shall be separable from the container without breaking the sterility of the container.

5.6.3.2   Containers for laboratory tests shall be properly labeled before the donation begins, shall accompany the blood container, and shall be reidentified with the blood container immediately after filling.

---

*FDA Memorandum, March 10, 1995, "Revision of FDA Memorandum of August 27, 1982: Requirements for Infrequent Plasmapheresis Donors."

FDA Memorandum, November 4, 1992, "Volume Limits for Automated Collection of Source Plasma."

FDA Guidance for Industry, February 13, 2001, "Technical Correction: Recommendations for Collecting Red Blood Cells by Automated Apheresis Methods."

5.6.3.3 Storage of samples before testing shall meet the requirements stated in the manufacturer's written instructions for the test being performed.

5.6.4 Ratio of Blood to Anticoagulant/Preservative Solution
The volume of blood to be collected shall be proportional to the amount of anticoagulant/preservative solution in the collection container.

5.6.5 Temperature During Transport
If blood is to be transported from the collection site to the component processing laboratory, it shall be placed in a qualified container having sufficient refrigeration capacity to cool the blood continuously toward a temperature range of 1 to 10 C until it arrives at the processing laboratory.

5.6.5.1 Blood intended for room temperature component preparation and Apheresis Platelets shall be transported and stored in a manner intended to cool the blood and Apheresis Platelets toward a temperature range of 20 to 24 C.

5.6.6 Additional Apheresis Collection Requirements

5.6.6.1 The process used in performing a phlebotomy and processing the blood shall be designed to ensure safe reinfusion of the autologous nonretained components.

5.6.6.2 Leukapheresis Collection
The collection facility shall have criteria for the administration and dose of any ancillary agents used.

5.6.6.2.1 Drugs to facilitate leukapheresis shall not be used for donors whose medical history suggests that such drugs may exacerbate a medical condition. The collection facility shall have a policy defining the maximal cumulative dose of any sedimenting agent that will be administered to a donor within a given time.

5.6.7 Therapeutic Phlebotomy and Apheresis
Therapeutic phlebotomy and apheresis shall be performed only when ordered by a physician.

5.6.7.1   Units drawn as therapeutic phlebotomies shall not be used for allogeneic transfusion unless one of the following conditions is met:

1)   The individual undergoing the therapeutic phlebotomy meets all allogeneic donor criteria and the unit is labeled with the disease/condition of the donor that makes phlebotomy necessary.

2)   The indication for therapeutic phlebotomy is hereditary hemochromatosis and the program has received variance approval from the FDA.*

5.7   Preparation/Processing of Components

Methods that ensure the quality and safety of components, including aliquots and pooled components, shall be employed.

5.7.1   Seal

If the seal is broken during processing, components shall be considered to have been prepared in an open system and expiration times specified for such components in Reference Standard 5.1.8A, Requirements for Storage, Transportation, and Expiration, apply.

5.7.2   Weld

If a sterile connection device is used to produce sterile welds between two pieces of compatible tubing, the following requirements shall apply:

5.7.2.1   The weld shall be inspected for completeness.

5.7.2.1.1   If the integrity of the weld is complete, the component shall retain original expiration dates or have storage times approved by the FDA.

5.7.2.1.2   If the integrity of the weld is incomplete, the container shall be considered an open system and may be sealed and used with a component expiration as indicated in Reference Standard 5.1.8A, Requirements for Storage, Transportation, and Expiration.

5.7.3   At the time of preparation of a final red-cell-containing component intended for transfusion, the integrally connected tubing shall be filled

*FDA Guidance, August 22, 2001, "Variances for Blood Collection from Individuals with Hereditary Hemochromatosis."

with an aliquot of the component and sealed in such a manner that it will be available for subsequent compatibility testing.

5.7.4   Methods

5.7.4.1   Leukocyte Reduction

Leukocyte-reduced blood and components shall be prepared by a method known to reduce the leukocyte number to <5 ×10^6 for Apheresis Platelets and Red Blood Cells and to <8.3 ×10^5 for whole-blood-derived Platelets. Validation and quality control shall demonstrate that at least 95% of units sampled meet this criterion.[*]

5.7.4.2   Irradiation

Irradiated blood and components shall be prepared by a method known to ensure that irradiation has occurred. A method shall be used to indicate that irradiation has occurred with each batch. The intended dose of irradiation shall be a minimum of 25 Gy (2500 cGy) delivered to the central portion of the container. The minimum dose at any point in the components shall be 15 Gy (1500 cGy). Alternate methods shall be demonstrated to be equivalent.[†]

5.7.4.2.1   Verification of dose delivery shall be performed using a fully loaded canister. Records shall be maintained as follows:
1) Annually for cesium-137 as a radiation source.
2) Semiannually for cobalt-60 as a radiation source.
3) Periodically, as recommended by the manufacturer for alternate sources of radiation.
4) Upon installation, major repairs, or relocation of the irradiator.

5.7.4.3   Pooling

For pooled components, the preparing facility shall maintain records of the ABO/Rh, donation identification number, and

---

[*]FDA Memorandum, May 29, 1996, "Recommendations and Licensure Requirements for Leukocyte-Reduced Blood Products."

[†]FDA Guidance, July 22, 1993, "Recommendations Regarding License Amendments and Procedures for Gamma Irradiation of Blood Products."

collecting facility for each unit in the pool. Standards 5.1.6.5.1 and 5.1.6.5.2 and Reference Standard 5.1.6A, Requirements for Labeling Blood and Components, apply.

5.7.5 Preparation of Specific Components

Reference Standard 5.1.8A, Requirements for Storage, Transportation, and Expiration, applies.

5.7.5.1 RED BLOOD CELLS (Red Blood Cells)

Red Blood Cells shall be prepared by separating the red cells from the plasma portion of blood.

5.7.5.1.1   Red Blood Cells without additive solutions shall be prepared using a method known to result in a final hematocrit of $\leq 80\%$.

5.7.5.2 FROZEN RED BLOOD CELLS (Red Blood Cells Frozen)

Frozen Red Blood Cells shall be prepared by a method known to minimize post-thaw hemolysis.

5.7.5.2.1   Red Blood Cells processed without additive solution shall be frozen within 6 days of collection, except when rejuvenated. Red Blood Cells processed with an additive solution shall be frozen before the expiration date of the Red Blood Cells.

5.7.5.3 REJUVENATED RED BLOOD CELLS (Red Blood Cells Rejuvenated)

Rejuvenated Red Blood Cells shall be prepared by following the manufacturer's written instructions. Rejuvenated Red Blood Cells shall be prepared by a method known to restore 2,3-diphosphoglycerate and adenosine triphosphate to normal levels or above. Reference Standard 5.1.8A, Requirements for Storage, Transportation, and Expiration, applies.

5.7.5.4 DEGLYCEROLIZED RED BLOOD CELLS (Red Blood Cells Deglycerolized)

Deglycerolized Red Blood Cells shall be prepared by a method known to ensure adequate removal of cryoprotective agents, result in minimal free hemoglobin in the supernatant solution, and yield a mean recovery of $\geq 80\%$ of the preglycerolization red cells following the deglycerolization process.

5.7.5.5   **WASHED RED BLOOD CELLS (Red Blood Cells Washed)**
Washed Red Blood Cells shall be prepared by a method known to ensure that the red cells are washed with a volume of compatible solution that will remove almost all of the plasma.

5.7.5.6   **RED BLOOD CELLS LEUKOCYTES REDUCED (Red Blood Cells Leukocytes Reduced)**
Red Blood Cells Leukocytes Reduced shall be prepared by a method known to retain at least 85% of the original red cells and contain $<5 \times 10^6$ residual leukocytes per unit. Standard 5.7.4.1 applies.

5.7.5.7   **RED BLOOD CELLS LOW VOLUME (Red Blood Cells Low Volume)**
When 300 to 404 mL of whole blood is collected into an anticoagulant volume calculated for 450 ± 45 mL or when 333 to 449 mL of whole blood is collected into an anticoagulant volume calculated for 500 ± 50 mL, red cells prepared from the resulting unit shall be labeled Red Blood Cells Low Volume. No other components shall be made from a low-volume collection.

5.7.5.8   **APHERESIS RED BLOOD CELLS (Red Blood Cells Pheresis)**
Apheresis Red Blood Cells shall be prepared by a method known to ensure a mean collection of ≥ 60 g of hemoglobin (or 180 mL red cell volume) per unit. At least 95% of the units sampled shall have >50 g of hemoglobin (or 150 mL red cell volume) per unit. Validation and quality control shall demonstrate that these criteria are met.

5.7.5.8.1   **APHERESIS RED BLOOD CELLS LEUKOCYTES REDUCED (Red Blood Cells Pheresis Leukocytes Reduced)**
Apheresis Red Blood Cells Leukocytes Reduced shall be prepared by a method known to ensure a final component containing a mean hemoglobin of ≥ 51 g (or 153 mL red cell volume) and $<5 \times 10^6$ residual leukocytes per unit. At least 95% of units

sampled shall have >42.5 g of hemoglobin (or 128 mL red cell volume). Standards 3.3 and 5.7.4.1 apply.

5.7.5.9 **FRESH FROZEN PLASMA (Fresh Frozen Plasma)**
Fresh Frozen Plasma shall be prepared from a whole blood or apheresis collection and placed at ≤−18 C within the time frame required for the anticoagulant or collection process.

5.7.5.9.1 If a liquid freezing bath is used, the container shall be protected from chemical alteration.

5.7.5.10 **PLASMA FROZEN WITHIN 24 HOURS AFTER PHLEBOTOMY (Plasma Frozen Within 24 Hours After Phlebotomy)**
Plasma Frozen Within 24 Hours After Phlebotomy shall be placed at ≤−18 C within 24 hours of collection.

5.7.5.10.1 If a liquid freezing bath is used, the container shall be protected from chemical alteration.

5.7.5.11 **LIQUID PLASMA (Liquid Plasma)**
Liquid Plasma shall be prepared by a method known to separate the plasma from the cellular components of the blood.

5.7.5.12 **THAWED PLASMA (Thawed Plasma)**
Thawed Plasma shall be prepared from Fresh Frozen Plasma or Plasma Frozen Within 24 Hours After Phlebotomy that has been collected in a closed system.

5.7.5.13 **RECOVERED PLASMA (Recovered Plasma)**
Recovered Plasma shall be prepared from donations originally intended for transfusion.

5.7.5.14 **CRYOPRECIPITATED AHF (Cryoprecipitated AHF)**
Cryoprecipitated AHF shall be prepared by a method known to separate the cold insoluble portion from Fresh Frozen Plasma and result in a minimum of 150 mg of fibrinogen and a minimum of 80 IU of coagulation Factor VIII per container or unit. In tests performed on pooled components, the pool shall contain a minimum of 150 mg of fibrinogen and 80 IU of coagulation Factor VIII times the number of components in the pool.

5.7.5.15   **PLASMA CRYOPRECIPITATE REDUCED (Plasma Cryoprecipitate Reduced)**
Plasma Cryoprecipitate Reduced shall be prepared by refreezing the supernatant plasma that has been used to prepare cryoprecipitate. It shall be refrozen within 24 hours of thawing the Fresh Frozen Plasma from which it was derived and stored at ≤-18 C.

5.7.5.16   **THAWED PLASMA CRYOPRECIPITATE REDUCED (Thawed Plasma Cryoprecipitate Reduced)**
Thawed Plasma Cryoprecipitate Reduced shall be prepared from Plasma Cryoprecipitate Reduced that has been collected in a closed system.

5.7.5.17   **PLATELETS (Platelets)**
Validation and quality control of Platelets from whole blood shall demonstrate that at least 90% of units sampled contain $\geq 5.5 \times 10^{10}$ platelets and have a pH ≥ 6.2 at the end of allowable storage. FDA criteria apply.[*]

5.7.5.18   **PLATELETS LEUKOCYTES REDUCED (Platelets Leukocytes Reduced)**
Validation and quality control of Platelets Leukocytes Reduced shall demonstrate that at least 75% of units sampled contain $\geq 5.5 \times 10^{10}$ platelets and at least 90% of units sampled have a pH ≥ 6.2 at the end of allowable storage. At a minimum, 95% of units sampled shall contain $<8.3 \times 10^{5}$ leukocytes. FDA criteria apply.[†]

5.7.5.19   **POOLED PLATELETS LEUKOCYTES REDUCED (Platelets Pooled Leukocytes Reduced)**
Pooled Platelets Leukocytes Reduced shall be prepared by a method known to result in a residual leukocyte count $<5 \times 10^{6}$. Standard 5.7.5.18 applies.

5.7.5.20   **APHERESIS PLATELETS (Platelets Pheresis)**
Validation and quality control of Apheresis Platelets shall demonstrate that at least 90% of units sampled contain ≥ 3.0

---

[*]21 CFR 640.25(b)(2) and 640.24(d).
[†]21 CFR 640.25(b)(2) and 640.24(d).

$\times 10^{11}$ platelets and, at the end of allowable storage or at the time of issue, have a pH $\geq$6.2. FDA criteria apply.[*]

5.7.5.21 APHERESIS PLATELETS LEUKOCYTES REDUCED (Platelets Pheresis Leukocytes Reduced)
Validation and quality control shall demonstrate that 90% of units sampled contain $\geq$3.0 $\times 10^{11}$ platelets and, at the end of allowable storage or at the time of issue, have a pH $\geq$6.2. FDA criteria apply.[†] At a minimum, 95% of units sampled shall contain a residual leukocyte count <5 $\times 10^6$.

5.7.5.22 APHERESIS GRANULOCYTES (Granulocytes Pheresis)
Unless prepared for neonates, Apheresis Granulocytes shall be prepared by a method known to yield a minimum of 1.0 $\times 10^{10}$ granulocytes in at least 75% of the units tested. Neonatal requirements shall be defined by the medical director.

5.8 Testing of Donor Blood

5.8.1 Determination of ABO Group for All Collections
The ABO group shall be determined for each collection by testing the red cells with anti-A and anti-B reagents and by testing the serum or plasma for expected antibodies with A_1 and B reagent red cells.

5.8.2 Determination of Rh Type for All Collections
The Rh type shall be determined for each collection with anti-D reagent. If the initial test with anti-D is negative, the blood shall be tested using a method designed to detect weak D. When either test is positive, the label shall read "Rh POSITIVE." When the tests for both D and weak D are negative, the label shall read "Rh NEGATIVE."

5.8.3 Detection of Unexpected Antibodies to Red Cell Antigens for Allogeneic Donors

5.8.3.1 Serum or plasma from donors with a history of transfusion or pregnancy shall be tested for unexpected antibodies to red cell antigens.

---

[*]21 CFR 640.25(b)(2).
[†]21 CFR 640.25(b)(2).

5.8.3.2 Methods for testing shall be those that demonstrate clinically significant red cell antibodies.[*]

5.8.3.3 A control system appropriate to the method of testing shall be used. Standard 5.1.3 applies.

5.8.4 Tests Intended to Prevent Disease Transmission by Allogeneic Donations
A sample of blood from each allogeneic donation shall be tested for HBsAg, anti-HBc, anti-HCV, HCV RNA, anti-HIV-1/2, HIV-1 RNA, anti-HTLV-I/II, a serologic test for syphilis and WNV RNA (seasonal criteria apply). Whole Blood and components shall not be distributed or issued for transfusion unless the results of these tests are negative, except in the case of a test for syphilis that has been shown to have a biological false-positive result. Units with biological false-positive results shall be labeled in accordance with FDA requirements. Standard 5.2.4 applies.[†]

5.8.4.1 If, due to urgent need, blood or components are distributed or issued before completion of these tests, a notation that testing is not completed shall appear conspicuously on an attached label or tie tag. Required tests shall be completed and results reported to the transfusion service as soon as possible.

5.8.4.2 For a cytapheresis donor dedicated to the support of a specific patient, testing required by Standard 5.8.4 shall be performed at the first donation and at least every 30 days thereafter.

5.8.5 Tests Intended to Prevent Disease Transmission by Autologous Donations
Autologous blood or components that will be transfused outside the collection facility shall be tested for HBsAg, anti-HBc, anti-HCV, HCV RNA, anti-HIV-1/2, HIV-1 RNA, anti-HTLV-I/II, WNV RNA (seasonal criteria apply), and a serologic test for syphilis. These tests shall be performed before shipping on at least the first unit collected during each 30-day period.[‡]

---

[*]21 CFR 606.151(d).
[†]FDA Memorandum, December 12, 1991, "Clarification of FDA Recommendations for Donor Deferral and Product Distribution Based on the Result of Syphilis Testing."
[‡]21 CFR 610.40(d).

5.8.5.1 The patient's physician and the patient shall be informed of any medically significant abnormalities discovered.[*]

5.8.6 Quarantine and Disposition of Units from Prior Collections
The blood bank or transfusion service shall have a process that is in accordance with FDA requirements and recommendations for quarantine and disposition of prior collections when a repeat donor has a reactive screening test for HBsAg, anti-HBc, anti-HCV, HCV RNA, anti-HIV-1/2, HIV-1 RNA, anti-HTLV-I/II, or WNV RNA.[†]

5.9 Final Labeling
The blood bank or transfusion service shall have a process to ensure that all specified requirements have been met at final labeling.

5.9.1 Testing and acceptability criteria shall be defined and there shall be evidence that all records relating to testing and acceptability criteria for the current donation, and the facility's deferral registry, have been reviewed.

5.9.2 The component shall be physically inspected for container integrity and normality of appearance.

5.9.3 ABO/Rh typing shall be compared to a historical type, if available. Discrepancies shall be resolved before release.

---

[*]21 CFR 630.6(d).

[†]21 CFR 610.46, 610.47, and 610.48.

FDA Memorandum, April 23, 1992, "Revised Recommendations for the Prevention of Human Immunodeficiency Virus (HIV) Transmission by Blood and Blood Products."

FDA Memorandum, July 19, 1996, "Recommendations for the Quarantine and Disposition of Units from Prior Collection from Donors with Repeatedly Reactive Screening Tests for Hepatitis B Virus (HBV), Hepatitis C Virus (HCV) and Human T Lymphotropic Virus Type I (HTLV-I)."

FDA Guidance for Industry, August 15, 1997, "Donor Screening for Antibodies to HTLV-II."

FDA Guidance for Industry, June 23, 2005, "Assessing Donor Suitability and Blood and Blood Product Safety in Cases of Known or Suspected West Nile Virus Infection."

FDA Guidance for Industry, August 24, 2007, "Lookback for Hepatitis C Virus (HCV): Product Quarantine, Consignee Notification, Further Testing, Product Disposition, and Notification of Transfusion Recipients Based on Donor Test Results Indicating Infection with HCV."

⌀   **5.9.4**   The facility shall ensure that blood and components from ineligible donors are quarantined and are not issued for transfusion.

  5.9.5   There shall be a method to confirm that the ABO/Rh label is correct. Confirmation shall be performed after the ABO and Rh label has been affixed to the units.

      5.9.5.1   When a computer system is used it shall be validated to prevent the release of ABO- and Rh-mislabeled components.

      5.9.5.2   The confirmation process shall be completed before release of Whole Blood and Red Blood Cell components.

5.10 Final Inspection

The blood bank or transfusion service shall have a process to ensure that blood, components, tissue, derivatives, or services meet specified requirements before distribution or issue.

<u>Transfusion-Service-Related Activities</u>

5.11 Samples and Requests

Identifying information for the patient and the blood sample shall correspond and be confirmed at the time of collection using two independent identifiers.

⌀   ### 5.11.1 Requests

Requests for blood, components, tests, tissue, and derivatives and records accompanying blood samples from the patient shall contain sufficient information to uniquely identify the patient, including two independent identifiers. The transfusion service shall accept only complete, accurate, and legible requests.

⌀   **5.11.1.1**   A physician or other authorized health professional shall order blood, components, tests, tissue, and derivatives.

5.11.2 Patient Samples

Blood samples shall be identified with an affixed label bearing sufficient information for unique identification of the patient, including two independent identifiers.

      5.11.2.1   The completed label shall be affixed to the tube before the person who drew the sample leaves the side of the patient.

5.11.2.2   There shall be a mechanism to identify the date of sample collection and the individual who drew the blood from the patient.

5.11.2.3   The transfusion service shall accept only those specimens that are completely, accurately, and legibly labeled.

5.11.3   Identifying Information

The transfusion service shall confirm that all identifying information on the request is in agreement with that on the sample label. In case of discrepancy or doubt, another sample shall be obtained.

5.11.4   Retention of Blood Samples

Patient samples and a segment from any red-cell-containing component shall be stored at refrigerated temperatures for at least 7 days after transfusion.

5.12   Serologic Confirmation of Donor Blood ABO/Rh (including autologous units)

Before transfusion, the ABO group of each Whole Blood and Red Blood Cell component and the Rh type of such units labeled as Rh negative shall be confirmed by a serologic test from an integrally attached segment. Confirmatory testing for weak D is not required.

5.12.1   Discrepancies shall be reported to the collecting facility and shall be resolved before issue of the blood for transfusion purposes.

5.13   Pretransfusion Testing of Patient Blood

Pretransfusion testing for allogeneic transfusion shall include ABO group, Rh type, and unexpected antibodies to red cell antigens.

5.13.1   ABO Group

The ABO group shall be determined by testing the red cells with anti-A and anti-B reagents and by testing the serum or plasma for expected antibodies with A_1 and B reagent red cells. If a discrepancy is detected and transfusion is necessary before resolution, only group O Red Blood Cells shall be issued.

5.13.2   Rh Type

Rh type shall be determined with anti-D reagent. The test for weak D is unnecessary when testing the patient.

5.13.3 Unexpected Antibodies to Red Cell Antigens

Methods of testing shall be those that demonstrate clinically significant antibodies. They shall include incubation at 37 C preceding an anti-globulin test using reagent red cells that are not pooled.

5.13.3.1 When clinically significant antibodies are detected, additional testing shall be performed.

5.13.3.2 If the patient has been transfused in the preceding 3 months with blood or a component containing allogeneic red cells, has been pregnant within the preceding 3 months, or if the history is uncertain or unavailable, a sample shall be obtained from the patient within 3 days of the scheduled transfusion. Day 0 is the day of draw.

5.13.3.3 In patients with previously identified clinically significant antibodies, methods of testing shall be those that identify additional clinically significant antibodies.

5.13.3.4 A control system appropriate to the method of testing shall be used. Standard 5.1.3 applies.

5.13.4 Pretransfusion Testing for Autologous Transfusion

Pretransfusion testing for autologous transfusion shall include ABO group and Rh type on the patient sample. Standard 5.12 applies.

5.13.5 Comparison with Previous Records

There shall be a process to ensure that 1) the historical records listed below have been reviewed and compared to current records, 2) discrepancies have been investigated, and 3) appropriate action has been taken before a unit is issued for transfusion.

5.13.5.1 ABO grouping and Rh typing performed during the past 12 months.

5.13.5.2 Difficulty in blood typing, clinically significant antibodies, significant adverse events to transfusion, and special transfusion requirements.

5.14 Selection of Compatible Blood and Components for Transfusion

5.14.1 Recipients shall receive ABO group-specific Whole Blood or ABO group-compatible Red Blood Cell components.

5.14.2 Rh-negative recipients shall receive Rh-negative Whole Blood or Red Blood Cell components.

5.14.2.1 The transfusion service shall have a policy for the use of Rh-positive red-cell-containing components in Rh-negative recipients. Standard 5.20 applies.

5.14.3 When clinically significant red cell antibodies are detected or the recipient has a history of such antibodies, Whole Blood or Red Blood Cell components shall be prepared for transfusion that do not contain the corresponding antigen and are serologically crossmatch-compatible.

5.14.4 The transfusion service shall have a policy concerning transfusion of components containing significant amounts of incompatible ABO antibodies or unexpected red cell antibodies.

5.14.5 The red cells in Apheresis Granulocytes and Platelets shall be ABO-compatible with the recipient's plasma and be crossmatched as in Standard 5.15 unless the component is prepared by a method known to result in a component containing <2 mL of red cells. The donor blood cells for the crossmatch may be obtained from a sample collected at the time of donation.

5.15 Crossmatch

5.15.1 Serologic Crossmatch
Before issue, a sample of the recipient's serum or plasma shall be crossmatched against a sample of donor cells from an integrally attached Whole Blood or Red Blood Cell segment. The crossmatch shall use methods that demonstrate ABO incompatibility and clinically significant antibodies to red cell antigens and shall include an antiglobulin test as described in Standard 5.13.3.

5.15.1.1 If no clinically significant antibodies were detected in tests performed in Standard 5.13.3 and there is no record of previous detection of such antibodies, at a minimum, detection of ABO incompatibility shall be performed.

5.15.2 Computer Crossmatch

If a computer system is used to detect ABO incompatibility, the following requirements shall be met:

5.15.2.1 The computer system has been validated on site to ensure that only ABO-compatible Whole Blood or Red Blood Cell components have been selected for transfusion.

5.15.2.2 Two determinations of the recipient's ABO group as specified in Standard 5.13.1 are made, one on a current sample and the second by one of the following methods: by retesting the same sample, by testing a second current sample, or by comparison with previous records. Standard 5.11 applies.

5.15.2.3 The system contains the donation identification number, component name, ABO group, and Rh type of the component; the confirmed unit ABO group; the two unique recipient identifiers; recipient ABO group, Rh type, and antibody screen results; and interpretation of compatibility.

5.15.2.4 A method exists to verify correct entry of data before release of blood or components.

5.15.2.5 The system contains logic to alert the user to discrepancies between the donor ABO group and Rh type on the unit label and those determined by blood group confirmatory tests and to ABO incompatibility between the recipient and the donor unit.

5.15.3 Preparation/Dispensing of Tissue

Before dispensing, for each tissue, any preparation steps that occur shall be performed according to the source facility's processes and procedures.

5.15.4 Preparation/Dispensing of Derivatives

Before dispensing, for each derivative, any preparation steps that occur shall be performed according to the source facility's processes and procedures.

5.16 Special Considerations for Neonates

5.16.1 An initial pretransfusion sample shall be tested to determine ABO group and Rh type. For ABO, only anti-A and anti-B reagents are required. The Rh type shall be determined as in Standard 5.13.2. The serum or plasma of either the neonate or the mother may be used to perform the test for unexpected antibodies as in Standard 5.13.3.

5.16.1.1 Repeat ABO grouping and Rh typing may be omitted for the remainder of the neonate's hospital admission or until the neonate reaches the age of 4 months, whichever is sooner.

5.16.1.2 If the initial screen for red cell antibodies is negative, it is unnecessary to crossmatch donor red cells for the initial or subsequent transfusions. Repeat testing may be omitted for the remainder of the neonate's hospital admission or until the neonate reaches the age of 4 months, whichever is sooner. Standard 5.16.2 applies.

5.16.1.3 If the initial antibody screen demonstrates clinically significant unexpected red cell antibodies, units shall be prepared for transfusion that either do not contain the corresponding antigen or are compatible by antiglobulin crossmatch until the antibody is no longer demonstrable in the neonate's serum or plasma.

5.16.2 If a non-group-O neonate is to receive non-group-O Red Blood Cells that are not compatible with the maternal ABO group, the neonate's serum or plasma shall be tested for anti-A or anti-B.

5.16.2.1 Test methods shall include an antiglobulin phase using either donor or reagent A_1 or B red cells. Standard 5.13.3.4 applies.

5.16.2.2 If anti-A or anti-B is detected, Red Blood Cells lacking the corresponding ABO antigen shall be transfused.

5.17 Selection of Compatible Blood and Components in Special Circumstances

Once it has been determined that a patient has special transfusion requirements, there shall be a mechanism to ensure that all future blood or components for that patient meet the special transfusion requirements for as long as clinically indicated.

5.17.1 Leukocyte-Reduced Components
The blood bank or transfusion service shall have a policy regarding transfusion of leukocyte-reduced components.

5.17.2 Cytomegalovirus
The blood bank or transfusion service shall have a policy regarding transfusion of cellular components selected or processed to reduce the risk of cytomegalovirus (CMV) transmission.

5.17.3 Irradiation
The blood bank or transfusion service shall have a policy regarding the transfusion of irradiated components.

 5.17.3.1 At a minimum, cellular components shall be irradiated when:

 5.17.3.1.1 A patient is identified as being at risk for transfusion-associated graft-vs-host disease.

 5.17.3.1.2 The donor of the component is a blood relative of the recipient.

 5.17.3.1.3 The donor is selected for HLA compatibility, by typing or crossmatching.

5.17.4 Hemoglobin S
The transfusion service shall have a policy regarding indications for the transfusion of Red Blood Cells or Whole Blood known to lack hemoglobin S.

5.17.5 Massive Transfusion
The transfusion service shall have a policy regarding compatibility testing when, within 24 hours, a patient has received an amount of blood approximating the total blood volume.

5.18 Final Inspection Before Issue
Blood, components, tissue, and derivatives shall be inspected at the time of issue. Standard 5.10 applies.

5.18.1 Transfusion Recipient Blood Container Identification
A blood container shall have an attached label or tie tag indicating:
1)   The intended recipient's two independent identifiers.

2) Donation identification number or pool number.
3) Interpretation of compatibility tests, if performed.

5.18.2 Issue of Blood and Components

At the time a unit is issued, there shall be a final check of transfusion service records and each unit of blood or component. Verification shall include:

1) The intended recipient's two independent identifiers, ABO group, and Rh type.
2) The donation identification number, the donor ABO group, and, if required, the Rh type.
3) The interpretation of crossmatch tests, if performed.
4) Special transfusion requirements.
5) The date and time of issue.

Standard 5.10 applies.

5.18.2.1 Issue of Tissue and Derivatives

The following information shall be verified:

1) The manufacturer's package insert documents are present and are issued.
2) Product quantity and name matches request.
3) The date and time of issue.
4) If tissue or derivatives are issued for a particular patient, the intended recipient's two independent identifiers.

5.18.3 The blood bank or transfusion service shall have a process to confirm agreement of the identifying information, the records, blood or component, and the request. Discrepancies shall be resolved before issue.

5.18.4 Reissue of Blood, Components, Tissue, and Derivatives

Blood, components, tissue, or derivatives that have been returned to the blood bank or transfusion service shall be reissued only if the following conditions have been observed:

1) The container closure has not been disturbed.
2) The appropriate temperature has been maintained.
3) For red cell components, at least one sealed segment of integral donor tubing has remained attached to the container. Removed segments shall be reattached only after confirming that the tubing identification numbers on both the removed segment(s) and the container are identical.
4) The records indicate that the blood, component, tissue, or derivative has been inspected and that it is acceptable for reissue.

5.18.5 Urgent Requirement for Blood and Components

The blood bank or transfusion service shall have a process for the provision of blood and components before completion of tests listed in Standards 5.8.4, 5.13.3, and 5.15 when a delay in transfusion could be detrimental to the patient. Standards 5.8.4.1, 5.12, and 7.0 to 7.2 apply.

5.18.5.1 Recipients whose ABO group is not known shall receive group O Red Blood Cells. Standard 5.13.1 applies.

5.18.5.2 If blood is issued before completion of compatibility testing, recipients whose ABO group has been determined as in Standard 5.13.1 by the transfusing facility shall receive only ABO group-specific Whole Blood or ABO group-compatible Red Blood Cell components.

5.18.5.3 The container tie tag or label shall indicate in a conspicuous fashion that compatibility and/or infectious disease testing was not completed at the time of issue.

5.18.5.4 Compatibility testing shall be completed expeditiously using a patient sample collected as early as possible in the transfusion sequence. Standard 5.17.5 applies.

5.18.5.5 The records shall contain a signed statement from the requesting physician indicating that the clinical situation was sufficiently urgent to require release of blood before completion of compatibility testing or infectious disease testing.

5.18.5.5.1 The transfusion service medical director and the recipient's physician shall be notified immediately of abnormal test results that may affect patient safety.

5.19 Administration of Blood and Components

There shall be a protocol for the administration of blood and components, including the use of infusion devices and ancillary equipment, and the identification, evaluation, and reporting of adverse events related to transfusion. The medical director shall participate in the development of these protocols. The protocol shall be consistent with the *Circular of Information for the Use of Human Blood and Blood Components*. Standard 7.4 applies.

5.19.1 Recipient Consent
The blood bank or transfusion service medical director shall participate in the development of policies, processes, and procedures regarding recipient consent for transfusion.

    5.19.1.1 At a minimum, elements of consent shall include all of the following:
1) A description of the risks, benefits, and treatment alternatives (including nontreatment).
2) The opportunity to ask questions.
3) The right to accept or refuse transfusion.

5.19.2 Transfusions shall be prescribed and administered under medical direction.

5.19.3 There shall be positive identification of the recipient using two independent identifiers.

5.19.4 Immediately before transfusion, the transfusionist shall verify that all information matching the blood or component with the intended recipient has been verified in the presence of the recipient, item by item.

5.19.5 All identification attached to the container shall remain attached until the transfusion has been terminated.

5.19.6 The patient's medical record shall include: transfusion order, documentation of patient consent, the name of the component, the donor identification number, the date and time of transfusion, pre- and post-transfusion vital signs, amount transfused, the identification of the transfusionist, and, if applicable, transfusion- related adverse events.

    5.19.6.1 For recipients of tissue, the recipient's medical record shall include the type of tissue, the numeric or alphanumeric identifier, the quantity, and the date of use.

    5.19.6.2 For recipients of derivatives, the recipient's medical record shall include product name, lot number, quantity, and administration date.

5.19.7 The patient shall be observed for potential adverse events during the transfusion and for an appropriate time thereafter. Standard 7.4 applies.

5.19.8 Specific written instructions concerning possible adverse events shall be provided to the patient or a responsible caregiver when direct medical observation or monitoring of the patient will not be available after transfusion.

5.19.9 Blood and components shall be transfused through a sterile, pyrogen-free transfusion set that has a filter designed to retain particles potentially harmful to the recipient.

5.19.10 Addition of Drugs and Solutions

With the exception of 0.9% sodium chloride (USP), drugs or medications shall not be added to blood or components unless one of the following conditions are met:
1) They have been approved for this use by the FDA.
2) There is documentation available to show that the addition is safe and does not adversely affect the blood or component.

5.19.11 Granulocytes

Leukocyte reduction filters or microaggregate filters shall not be used. Standard 5.19.9 applies.

5.20 Rh Immune Globulin

The transfusion service shall have a policy for Rh Immune Globulin prophylaxis for Rh-negative patients who have been exposed to Rh-positive red cells.

5.20.1 Interpretation criteria shall be established to prevent the mistyping of an Rh-negative patient as Rh positive due to exposure to Rh-positive red cells.

5.20.2 Women who are pregnant or who have been pregnant recently shall be considered for Rh Immune Globulin administration when all of the following apply:
1) The woman's test for D antigen is negative. A test for weak D is not required.
2) The woman is not known to be actively immunized to the D antigen.
3) The Rh type of the fetus/infant is unknown or the type of the fetus/infant is positive when tested for D or weak D. Weak D testing is required when the test for D is negative.

5.20.3 There shall be a process to ensure that an adequate dose of Rh Immune Globulin is administered.

5.20.4 Rh Immune Globulin shall be administered as soon as possible after exposure.

5.20.5 Patients who have received Rh Immune Globulin shall be evaluated for additional treatment for any subsequent sensitizing events.

Reference Standard 5.1.6A—Requirements for Labeling Blood and Components

Item No.	Labeling Item	Collection or Preparation	Final Component	Pooled
1	Name of blood component, intended component, or tissue[1]	NR	R	R
2	Donation identification number[1]	R	R	R
3	Identity of anticoagulant[2] or other preservative solution	R	R	R
4	Identity of sedimenting agent, if applicable	NR	R	NA
5	Approximate volume[3]	NR	R	R, total
6	Facility collecting component[1]	NR	R	NR
7	Facility modifying component[4]	NA	R, if leaves the facility	R[1]
8	Storage temperature	NA	R	R
9	Expiration date and, when appropriate, time	NA	R	R
10	ABO group and Rh type[1,5]	NA	R	see item 18
11	Specificity of unexpected red cell antibodies[6]	NA	R[2]	R
12	Instructions to the transfusionist 1. "See *Circular of Information for the Use of Human Blood and Blood Components*" 2. "Properly identify intended recipient" 3. "This product may transmit infectious agents" 4. "Rx Only"	NR	R	R
13	Phrase: "Volunteer Donor," if applicable	NR	R	R

#				
14	Phrase: "Paid Donor," if applicable	R	R	R
15	CMV seronegative, if applicable	NR	R	R
16	Indication that the unit is low volume, and the actual volume, if applicable	NR	R	NA
17	Number of units in pool[6]	NA	NA	R
18	ABO and Rh of units in pool[5,7]	NA	NA	R
Additional Autologous Labeling Requirements				
19	Phrase: "For autologous use only"	R	R	R
20	Phrase: "Autologous Donor," if applicable[6]	R	R	R
21	Recipient name, identification number, and, if available, name of facility where patient is to be transfused[6]	R	R	R
22	Biohazard label, if applicable[8]	NR	R	R
23	Phrase "Donor untested," if applicable[9]	NR	R	NA
24	Phrase "Donor tested within the last 30 days," if applicable[10]	NR	R	NA
Additional Dedicated Donor Labeling Requirements				
25	Intended recipient information label	R	R	NA
26	Donor tested within the last 30 days, if applicable[10]	NR	R	NA

(Continued)

Reference Standard 5.1.6A–Requirements for Labeling Blood and Components (Continued)

Item No.	Labeling Item	Collection or Preparation	Final Component	Pooled
	Labeling Requirements for Recovered Plasma[11]			
27	"Caution: For Manufacturing Use Only"	NA	R	R
28	Biohazard label, if applicable	NR	R	R
29	"Not for use in Products Subject to License Under Section 351 of the Public Health Service Act" (Applicable to plasma not meeting requirements for manufacture into licensable products)	NA	R	R
30	In lieu of expiration date, the date of collection of the oldest material in the container	R	R	R

R = Required; NR = Not Required; NA = Not Applicable

[1]Must be machine-readable (see Standard 5.1.6.3.1).

[2]Not required for Cryoprecipitated AHF or frozen, deglycerolized, rejuvenated, or washed Red Blood Cells.

[3]For platelets, low-volume Red Blood Cells, Fresh Frozen Plasma, pooled components, and components prepared by apheresis, the approximate volume in the container.

[4]Includes irradiation, if applicable.

[5]Rh type not required for cryoprecipitate.

[6]The facility has the option of putting information on a tie tag or label. Specificity of antibodies is not required for autologous units that are not crossed over.

[7]For pooled cryoprecipitate, plasma, or platelets of mixed types, a pooled type label is acceptable. The specific ABO group and Rh types of units in the pool may be put on a tie tag. Standard 5.7.4.3 applies.

[8]Biohazard labels for autologous units shall be used for the following test results:

Reference Standard 5.1.6A—Requirements for Labeling Blood and Components (Continued)

Test	Test Result
HBsAg	Repeatedly reactive
Anti-HBc	Repeatedly reactive
Anti-HCV	Repeatedly reactive
HCV NAT	Positive or reactive
Anti-HIV-1/2	Repeatedly reactive
HIV-1 NAT	Positive or reactive
Anti-HTLV-I/II	Repeatedly reactive
Syphilis	Reactive
When performed:	
HBV NAT	Positive or reactive
WNV NAT	Positive or reactive
Chagas' antibody screening	Repeatedly reactive

[9]Donor not tested for evidence of infectious diseases.
[10]When the first unit has been tested but any unit collected within 30 days after the first collection has not been tested.
[11]Labeling of Recovered Plasma shall conform to 21 CFR 606.121(e)(5) and 21 CFR 610.40(h)(2)(ii).

Reference Standard 5.1.8A—Requirements for Storage, Transportation, and Expiration

Item No.	Component	Storage	Transport	Expiration[1]	Additional Criteria
Whole Blood Components					
1	Whole Blood	1-6 C. If intended for room temperature components, then store at 1-6 C within 8 hours	Cooling toward 1-10 C. If intended for room temperature components, cooling toward 20-24 C	ACD/CPD/CP2D: 21 days CPDA-1: 35 days	
2	Whole Blood Irradiated	1-6 C	1-10 C	Original expiration or 28 days from date of irradiation, whichever is sooner	
Red Blood Cell Components					
3	Red Blood Cells	1-6 C	1-10 C	ACD/CPD/CP2D: 21 days CPDA-1: 35 days Additive solution: 42 days Open system: 24 hours	
4	Deglycerolized RBCs	1-6 C	1-10 C	Open system: 24 hours or as FDA approved Closed system: 14 days or as FDA approved	

5	Frozen RBCs 40% Glycerol	≤-65 C if 40% Glycerol or as FDA approved	Maintain frozen state	10 years (A policy shall be developed if rare frozen units are to be retained beyond this time)	Closed system: Frozen within 6 days Open system: Frozen within 6 days of collection without an additive; frozen before RBC expiration if with an additive approved for this purpose
6	RBCs Irradiated	1-6 C	1-10 C	Original expiration or 28 days from date of irradiation, whichever is sooner	
7	RBCs Leukocytes Reduced	1-6 C	1-10 C	ACD/CPD/CP2D: 21 days CPDA-1: 35 days Additive solution: 42 days Open system: 24 hours	
8	Rejuvenated RBCs	1-6 C	1-10 C	CPD, CPDA-1: 24 hours AS-1: freeze after rejuvenation	Follow manufacturer's written instructions

(Continued)

Reference Standard 5.1.8A—Requirements for Storage, Transportation, and Expiration (Continued)

Item No.	Component	Storage	Transport	Expiration[1]	Additional Criteria
9	Deglycerolized Rejuvenated RBCs	1-6 C	1-10 C	24 hours or as approved by FDA	Follow manufacturer's written instructions
10	Frozen Rejuvenated RBCs	≤-65 C	Maintain frozen state	CPD, CPDA-1: 10 years AS-1: 3 years (A policy shall be developed if rare frozen units are to be retained beyond this time)	Follow manufacturer's written instructions
11	Washed RBCs	1-6 C	1-10 C	24 hours	
12	Apheresis RBCs	1-6 C	1-10 C	CPDA-1: 35 days Additive solution: 42 days Open system: 24 hours	
13	Apheresis RBCs Leukocytes Reduced	1-6 C	1-10 C	CPDA-1: 35 days Additive solution: 42 days Open system: 24 hours	

Platelet Components

#	Component	Storage	Transport	Expiration	Maximum time without agitation
14	Platelets	20-24 C with continuous gentle agitation	20-24 C (as close as possible to)	24 hours to 5 days, depending on collection system	Maximum time without agitation 24 hours
15	Platelets Irradiated	20-24 C with continuous gentle agitation	20-24 C (as close as possible to)	No change from original expiration date	Maximum time without agitation 24 hours
16	Platelets Leukocytes Reduced	20-24 C with continuous gentle agitation	20-24 C (as close as possible to)	Open system: 4 hours Closed system: No change in expiration	Maximum time without agitation 24 hours
17	Pooled Platelets Leukocytes Reduced	20-24 C with continuous gentle agitation	20-24 C (as close as possible to)	Open system: within 4 hours of opening the system Closed system: 4 hours after pooling or 5 days following collection[2]	Maximum time without agitation 24 hours
18	Pooled Platelets (or open system)	20-24 C with continuous gentle agitation	20-24 C (as close as possible to)	Open system: 4 hours	
19	Apheresis Platelets	20-24 C with continuous gentle agitation	20-24 C (as close as possible to)	24 hours to 5 days, depending on collection system	Maximum time without agitation 24 hours

(Continued)

Reference Standard 5.1.8A—Requirements for Storage, Transportation, and Expiration (Continued)

Item No.	Component	Storage	Transport	Expiration[1]	Additional Criteria
20	Apheresis Platelets Irradiated	20-24 C with continuous gentle agitation	20-24 C (as close as possible to)	No change from original expiration date	Maximum time without agitation 24 hours
21	Apheresis Platelets Leukocytes Reduced	20-24 C with continuous gentle agitation	20-24 C (as close as possible to)	Open system: within 4 hours of opening the system Closed system: 5 days	Maximum time without agitation 24 hours
Granulocyte Components					
22	Apheresis Granulocytes	20-24 C	20-24 C (as close as possible to)	24 hours	Transfuse as soon as possible
23	Apheresis Granulocytes Irradiated	20-24 C	20-24 C (as close as possible to)	No change from original expira-tion date	Transfuse as soon as possible
Plasma Components					
24	Cryoprecipitated AHF	$\leq$-18 C	Maintain frozen state	12 months from original collection	Thaw the FFP at 1-6 C Place cryoprecipitate in the freezer within 1 hour

25	Pooled Cryoprecipitated AHF (before freezing)	≤–18C	Maintain frozen state	12 months from earliest date of collection of product in pool	If Rh-positive units and Rh-negative units are pooled together, the pooled unit shall be labeled either as Rh positive or as pooled Rh. Diluents shall not be used before freezing.
26	Cryoprecipi-tated AHF (after thawing)	20-24 C	20-24 C (as close as possible to)	Open system or pooled: 4 hours Single unit: 6 hours	Thaw at 30-37 C When diluent is needed, 0.9% sodium chloride (USP) may be added.
27	Fresh Frozen Plasma (FFP)	≤–18 C or ≤–65 C	Maintain frozen state	<–18 C: 12 months <–65 C: 7 years	Place in freezer within 8 hours of collection in CPD, CP2D, CPDA-1, or within 6 hours of collection in ACD or as

(Continued)

Reference Standard 5.1.8A—Requirements for Storage, Transportation, and Expiration (Continued)

Item No.	Component	Storage	Transport	Expiration[1]	Additional Criteria
27 (cont)	Fresh Frozen Plasma (FFP)	$\leq$-18 C or $\leq$-65 C	Maintain frozen state	<-18 C: 12 months <-65 C: 7 years	FDA-cleared. Storage at <-65 C requires FDA approval if product is stored for longer than 12 months.
28	FFP (after thawing)	1-6 C	1-10 C	If issued as FFP: 24 hours	Thaw at 30-37 C or by using an FDA-cleared device
29	Plasma Frozen Within 24 Hours After Phlebotomy	$\leq$-18 C	Maintain frozen state	12 months	Place in freezer within 24 hours of collection
30	Plasma Frozen Within 24 Hours After Phlebotomy (after thawing)	1-6 C	1-10 C	If issued as FP24: 24 hours	Thaw at 30-37 C or by using an FDA-cleared device
31	Thawed Plasma	1-6 C	1-10 C	5 days from date original product was thawed	Shall have been collected in a closed system

#	Component				
32	Plasma Cryoprecipitate Reduced	≤−18 C	Maintain frozen state	12 months	
33	Plasma Cryoprecipitate Reduced (after thawing)	1-6 C	1-10 C	24 hours	Thaw at 30-37 C
34	Thawed Plasma Cryoprecipitate Reduced	1-6 C	1-10 C	5 days	Shall have been collected in a closed system
35	Liquid Plasma	1-6 C	1-10 C	5 days after expiration of Whole Blood	21 CFR 640.34(c) applies
36	Recovered Plasma, liquid or frozen	Refer to short supply agreement	Refer to short supply agreement	Refer to short supply agreement	Requires a short supply agreement[3]

Tissue and Derivatives

#	Component				
37	Tissue	Conform to source facility's written instructions	Conform to source facility's written instructions	Conform to source facility's written instructions	
38	Derivatives	Conform to manufacturer's written instructions	Conform to manufacturer's written instructions	Conform to manufacturer's written instructions	

[1] If the seal is broken during processing, components stored at 1 to 6 C shall have an expiration time of 24 hours and components stored at 20 to 24 C shall have an expiration time of 4 hours, unless otherwise indicated.
[2] Storage beyond 4 hours requires an FDA-cleared system.
[3] 21 CFR 601.22.

Reference Standard 5.4.1A—Requirements for Allogeneic Donor Qualification*

Category	Criteria/Description/Examples	Deferral Period
1) Age	• Conform to applicable state law or • 16 years	
2) Whole Blood Volume Collected	• Maximum of 10.5 mL/kg of donor weight, including samples	
3) Donation Interval	• 8 weeks after whole blood donation (Standards 5.5.1 to 5.5.4 and 5.6.7.1 apply) • 16 weeks after 2-unit red cell collection • 4 weeks after infrequent plasmapheresis • ≥2 days after plasma-, platelet-, or leukapheresis	
4) Temperature	• ≤37.5 C (99.5 F) if measured orally, or equivalent if measured by another method	
5) Hemoglobin/Hematocrit	• ≥12.5 g/dL/>38%; blood obtained by earlobe puncture shall not be used for this determination • For 2-unit Red Blood Cell collections, follow operator's manual for instrument	
6) Drug Therapy	Generic medication name (trade name)	
	• Finasteride (Proscar, Propecia), isotretinoin (Accutane, Amnesteem, Claravis, Sotret)	1 month after last dose
	• Dutasteride (Avodart)	6 months after last dose
	• Acitretin (Soriatane)	3 years after last dose
	• Etretinate (Tegison)	Permanent
	• Bovine insulin manufactured in the United Kingdom	Indefinite

	Medications that irreversibly inhibit platelet function preclude use of the donor as sole source of platelets	
	a. Aspirin and piroxicam (Feldene)	a. 2 full days (>48 hours) after last dose
	b. Clopidogrel (Plavix) and Ticlopidine (Ticlid)	b. 14 days after last dose
	• Warfarin (Coumadin), for plasma products for transfusion	One week (7 days) after last dose
	• Other medications, such as antibiotics	As defined by the facility's medical director
7) Medical History and General Health	• The prospective donor shall appear to be in good health and shall be free of major organ disease (eg, heart, liver, lungs), cancer, or abnormal bleeding tendency, unless determined eligible by the medical director	
	• The venipuncture site shall be evaluated for lesions on the skin. The venipuncture site shall be free from infectious skin disease and any disease that might create a risk of contaminating the blood	
	• Family history of Creutzfeldt-Jakob disease (CJD)[1]	Indefinite deferral for risk of CJD
8) Pregnancy	• Defer if pregnant within the last 6 weeks	
9) Receipt of Blood, Component, or Other Human Tissue	• Receipt of dura mater or pituitary growth hormone of human origin	Indefinite
	• Receipt of blood, components, human tissue, or plasma-derived clotting factor concentrates	12 months

(Continued)

Reference Standard 5.4.1A—Requirements for Allogeneic Donor Qualification* (Continued)

Category	Criteria/Description/Examples	Deferral Period
10) Immunizations and Vaccinations	• Receipt of toxoids, or synthetic or killed viral, bacterial, or rickettsial vaccines if donor is symptom-free and afebrile [Anthrax, Cholera, Diphtheria, Hepatitis A, Hepatitis B, Influenza, Lyme disease, Paratyphoid, Pertussis, Plague, Pneumococcal polysaccharide, Polio (Salk/injection), Rabies, Rocky Mountain spotted fever, Tetanus, Typhoid (by injection)] • Receipt of recombinant vaccine (eg, HPV vaccine)	None
	• Receipt of live attenuated viral and bacterial vaccines [Measles (rubeola), Mumps, Polio (Sabin/oral), Typhoid (oral), Yellow fever]	2 weeks
	• Receipt of live attenuated viral and bacterial vaccines [German measles (rubella), Chicken pox (varicella zoster)]	4 weeks
	• Smallpox[2]	Refer to FDA Guidance
	• Receipt of other vaccines, including unlicensed vaccines	12 months unless otherwise indicated by medical director
11) Infectious Diseases	• History of viral hepatitis after 11th birthday	Indefinite
	• Confirmed positive test for HBsAg	Permanent
	• Repeatedly reactive test for anti-HBc on more than one occasion	Indefinite
	• Present or past clinical or laboratory evidence of infection with HIV, HCV, HTLV or as excluded by current FDA regulations and recommendations for the prevention of HIV transmission by blood and components	Indefinite

• A history of babesiosis, or Chagas' disease	Indefinite
• Evidence or obvious stigmata of parenteral drug use	Indefinite
• Use of a needle to administer nonprescription drugs	Indefinite
• Mucous membrane exposure to blood	12 months
• Nonsterile skin penetration with instruments or equipment contaminated with blood or body fluids other than the donor's own. Includes tattoos or permanent make-up unless applied by a state-regulated entity with sterile needles and ink that has not been reused.	12 months
• Sexual contact or lived with an individual who: a. Has acute or chronic hepatitis B (positive HBsAg test, HBV NAT) b. Has symptomatic hepatitis C c. Is symptomatic for any other viral hepatitis	12 months
• Sexual contact with an individual with HIV infection or at high risk of HIV infection[3,4]	12 months
Incarceration in a correctional institution (including juvenile detention, lockup, jail, or prison) for more than 72 consecutive hours	12 months
Syphilis or gonorrhea[5] a. Following the diagnosis of syphilis or gonorrhea. Must have completed treatment. b. Donor who has a reactive screening test for syphilis where no confirmatory testing was performed c. A confirmed positive test for syphilis (FDA reentry protocol applies)	12 months (in accordance with FDA Guidance)

(Continued)

Reference Standard 5.4.1A—Requirements for Allogeneic Donor Qualification* (Continued)

Category	Criteria/Description/Examples	Deferral Period
	• West Nile virus	In accordance with FDA Guidance[6]
	• Malaria These deferral periods apply irrespective of the receipt of antimalarial prophylaxis a. Prospective donors who have had a diagnosis of malaria	a. 3 years after becoming asymptomatic
	b. Individual(s) who have lived for at least 5 consecutive years in areas considered malaria-endemic by the Malarial Branch, Centers for Disease Control and Prevention, US Department of Health and Human Services	b. 3 years after departure from malaria-endemic area(s)
	c. Individuals who have traveled to an area where malaria is endemic[7,8]	c. Defer for 12 months after departing that area
12) Travel	The prospective donor's travel history shall be evaluated for potential risks[1,7]	
	Donors recommended for indefinite deferral for risk of vCJD, as defined in most recent FDA Guidance[1]	Defer indefinitely

* For blood pressure, see 21 CFR 640.3(b)(2).

[1]FDA Guidance for Industry, January 9, 2002, "Revised Preventive Measures to Reduce the Possible Risk of Transmission of Creutzfeldt-Jakob Disease (CJD) and Variant Creutzfeldt-Jakob Disease (vCJD) by Blood and Blood Products."

[2]FDA Guidance for Industry, December 30, 2002, "Recommendations for Deferral of Donors and Quarantine and Retrieval of Blood and Blood Products in Recent Recipients of Smallpox Vaccine (Vaccinia Virus) and Certain Contacts of Smallpox Vaccine Recipients."

[3]FDA Memorandum, April 23, 1992, "Revised Recommendation for the Prevention of Human Immunodeficiency Virus (HIV) Transmission by Blood and Blood Products."

[4]FDA Memorandum, December 11, 1996, "Interim Recommendations for Deferral of Donors at Increased Risk for HIV-1 Group O Infection."

[5]FDA Memorandum, December 12, 1991, "Clarification of FDA Recommendations for Donor Deferral and Product Distribution Based on the Results of Syphilis Testing."

[6]FDA Guidance for Industry, June 23, 2005, "Assessing Donor Suitability and Blood and Blood Product Safety in Cases of Known or Suspected West Nile Virus Infection."

[7]www.cdc.gov/travel.

6. DOCUMENTS AND RECORDS

6.0 Documents and Records

The blood bank or transfusion service shall have policies, processes, and procedures to ensure that documents are identified, reviewed, approved, and retained and that records are created, stored, and archived in accordance with record retention policies.

6.1 Documents

The blood bank or transfusion service shall have a process for document control that includes the following elements:

6.1.1 A master list of documents, including policies, processes, procedures, labels, and forms that relate to the requirements of these *BB/TS Standards*.

6.1.2 Use of standardized formats for all policies, processes, and procedures. Additional procedures (such as those in an operator's manual or published in the AABB *Technical Manual*) may be incorporated by reference.

6.1.3 Review and approval of new and revised documents before use.

6.1.4 Annual review of each policy, process, and procedure by an authorized individual.

6.1.5 Use of only current and valid documents. Appropriate and applicable documents shall be available at all locations where activities essential to meeting the requirements of these *BB/TS Standards* are performed.

6.1.6 Identification and appropriate archival of obsolete documents.

6.2 Records

The blood bank or transfusion service shall ensure identification, collection, indexing, access, filing, storage, and disposition of records as required by Reference Standards 6.2A through 6.2E, Retention of Records.

6.2.1 Facility Records

Records shall be complete, retrievable in a period appropriate to the circumstances, and protected from accidental or unauthorized destruction or modification.

6.2.1.1 Copies

Before the destruction of the original records, the blood bank or transfusion service shall have a process to ensure that copies of records are identified as such. Copies of records shall be verified as containing the original content and shall be legible, complete, and accessible.

6.2.2

A system designed to prevent unauthorized access and ensure confidentiality of records shall be established and followed.

6.2.3

The record system shall make it possible to trace any unit of blood, component, tissue, or derivative from its source to final disposition; to review the records applying to the specific component; and to investigate adverse events manifested by the recipient.

6.2.3.1

The system shall ensure that the donor and patient identifiers are unique.

6.2.4

Records shall be created concurrently with performance of each critical activity.

6.2.4.1

The actual result of each test performed shall be recorded immediately and the final interpretation shall be recorded upon completion of testing.

6.2.5 Electronic Records

There shall be processes and procedures to support the management of computer systems.

6.2.5.1

There shall be a process in place for routine backup of all critical data.

6.2.5.1.1

Procedures shall be in place to ensure that data are retrievable and usable.

6.2.5.1.2

Backup data shall be stored in an off-site location.

Reference Standard 6.2A–Retention of Donor/Unit Records

Item No.	Standard	Record to Be Maintained	Minimum Retention Time (in years)[1,2]
1	4.3	Inspection of incoming blood and components	10
2	5.1.6.1	Identification of individuals performing each significant step in collection, processing, compatibility testing, and transportation of blood and components	10
3	5.1.6.2	Traceability of blood, components, tissue, derivatives, and critical materials	10
4	5.1.6.5	Source to final disposition of each unit of blood or blood component and, if issued by the facility for transfusion, identification of the recipient	10
5	5.1.6.5.1, 5.1.6.5.2	Unique identification of each unit	10
6	5.2.1 #3	Donor acknowledgment that educational materials have been read	10
7	5.2.2	Parental permission for donation	10
8	5.2.3	Consent of donors	10
9	5.2.4	Notification to donor of significant abnormal findings	10
10	5.2.4	Donors placed on permanent deferral, and indefinite deferral for protection of recipient	Indefinite
11	5.4.1 5.4.2	Donor information, including address, medical history, physical examination, health history, or other conditions thought to compromise suitability of blood or component	10
12	5.4.4.1	A medical order from the patient's physician is required to collect blood for autologous use	10

Reference Standard 6.2A—Retention of Donor/Unit Records (Continued)

Item No.	Standard	Record to Be Maintained	Minimum Retention Time (in years)[1,2]
13	5.5.3.4	Platelet count for frequent plateletpheresis donors	10
14	5.6.6	Cytapheresis record, including anticoagulant drugs given, duration of procedure, volume of components, drugs used, lot number of disposables, and replacement fluids	10
15	5.6.6.2.1	Maximal cumulative dose of sedimenting agent administered to donor in a given time	10
16	5.7.2.1	Inspection of weld for completeness and identification numbers of blood or components and of lot numbers of disposables used during component preparation	10
17	5.7.4.2.1	Verification of irradiation dose delivery	10
18	5.7.4.3	Donation identification number and collecting facility for each unit in pooled components	10
19	5.7.5	Preparation of specific components	10
20	5.8.1, 5.8.2	ABO group and Rh type for all collections	10
21	5.8.3.1	Allogeneic donor testing to detect unexpected antibodies to red cell antigens for donors with history of transfusion or pregnancy	10
22	5.8.3.3	Use of a control system appropriate to the method of testing	10
23	5.8.4	Interpretations of disease marker testing for allogeneic testing	10

(Continued)

Reference Standard 6.2A—Retention of Donor/Unit Records (Continued)

Item No.	Standard	Record to Be Maintained	Minimum Retention Time (in years)[1,2]
24	5.8.4.1	Distribution or issue of units before completion of tests	10
25	5.8.6	Quarantine of units from prior collections when a repeat donor has a reactive disease marker screening test	10
26	5.9.1	Final review of records relating to testing and acceptability criteria	10
27	5.9.4	Review of donor records to ensure any units from an ineligible donor are quarantined	10
28	5.12	Serologic confirmation of donor blood ABO/Rh	10
29	5.12.1	Reporting and resolution of ABO donor ABO/Rh discrepancies to collecting facility	10
30	5.18.4	If a unit is returned for reissue, confirmation that the tubing identification number on reattached segments is identical and confirmation that the blood or components has been inspected and is acceptable	10
31	5.18.5.5	The records shall contain a signed statement from the requesting physician indicating that the clinical situation was sufficiently urgent to require release of blood before completion of compatibility testing or infectious disease testing	10
32	7.1.4	Blood and components that are determined after release not to conform to specified requirements	10
33	7.3	Adverse events related to donation	10

Reference Standard 6.2A—Retention of Donor/Unit Records (Continued)

Item No.	Standard	Record to Be Maintained	Minimum Retention Time (in years)[1,2]
34	7.4.5.2	Collection facility report of the investigation of transfusion-transmitted disease	10
35	7.4.6	Look-back investigation	10

[1]Applicable state or local law may exceed this period.
[2]21 CFR 606.160(d).

Reference Standard 6.2B—Retention of Patient Records

Item No.	Standard	Record to Be Maintained	Minimum Retention Time (in years)[1,2]
1	5.1.6.5	Source to final disposition of each unit of blood or blood component and, if issued by the facility for transfusion, identification of the recipient	10
2	5.4.4.5	Approval by medical director authorizing the transfusion of autologous blood to allogeneic recipient	5
3	5.6.7	*Therapeutic apheresis:* patient identification, diagnosis, type of therapeutic procedure performed, method used, vital signs before and after the procedure, extracorporeal blood volume if applicable, nature and volume of component removed, nature and volume of replacement fluids, any occurrence of adverse events, and medication administered *Therapeutic phlebotomy:* patient identification, diagnosis, vital signs before the procedure, volume removed, and occurrence of adverse events	5
4	5.11.1	Requests for blood and components	5
5	5.11.1.1	Order for blood, components, tests, and derivatives	5
6	5.13.1, 5.13.2	Test results and interpretation of patient's ABO group and Rh type	10
7	5.13.3	Patient testing to detect unexpected antibodies to red cell antigens	10
8	5.13.3.1	Additional testing to detect clinically significant antibodies	10

Reference Standard 6.2B—Retention of Patient Records (Continued)

Item No.	Standard	Record to Be Maintained	Minimum Retention Time (in years)[1,2]
9	5.13.3.4	Use of a control system appropriate to the method of testing	5
10	5.13.4	ABO/Rh testing for autologous transfusion	5
11	5.13.5	Comparison of patient's previous test results for ABO group and Rh type in last 12 months, if comparison is not performed electronically	5
12	5.13.5.1	Comparison of ABO grouping and Rh typing during the last 12 months; investigation and resolution of discrepancies	5
13	5.13.5.2	Difficulty in typing, clinically significant antibodies, significant adverse events to transfusions, and special transfusion requirements; investigation and resolution of discrepancies	Indefinite
14	5.15.1	Test results and interpretation of serologic crossmatch	10
15	5.15.1.1	Detection of ABO incompatibility when no clinically significant antibodies are detected	10
16	5.15.2.2	Two determinations of the recipient's ABO group	10
17	5.15.2.3	Interpretation of computer crossmatch	10
18	5.16.1	ABO/Rh of neonatal recipients	10
19	5.16.1.3	Selection of compatible units when initial antibody screen for neonates demonstrates clinically significant antibodies	10

(Continued)

Reference Standard 6.2B—Retention of Patient Records (Continued)

Item No.	Standard	Record to Be Maintained	Minimum Retention Time (in years)[1,2]
20	5.16.2	Testing of neonate's serum or plasma shall be tested for anti-A or anti-B if a non-group-O neonate is to receive non-group-O Red Blood Cells that are not compatible with the maternal ABO group	10
21	5.17.3.1.1, 5.17.3.1.2, 5.17.3.1.3	Irradiation of cellular components, if applicable	10
22	5.18	Final inspection of blood and components before issue; if the container is not intact or components are abnormal in appearance, maintain record of medical director approval	10
23	5.18.2	Final check of transfusion service records at issue	10
24	5.18.5.5	A signed statement from the requesting physician indicating that the clinical situation was sufficiently urgent to require release of blood before completion of compatibility testing or infectious disease testing	10
25	5.18.5.5.1	Notification of abnormal test results	10
26	5.19.1	Recipient consent	5
27	5.19.4	Verification of patient identification before transfusion	5

Reference Standard 6.2B—Retention of Patient Records (Continued)

Item No.	Standard	Record to Be Maintained	Minimum Retention Time (in years)[1,2]
28	5.19.6, 7.4	Patient's medical record: transfusion order, documentation of patient consent, component name, donation identification number, date and time of transfusion, pre-and posttransfusion vital signs, the amount transfused, identification of the transfusionist, and, if applicable, transfusion-related adverse event(s)	5
29	7.4.1.2	Immediate evaluation of suspected transfusion reactions	5
30	7.4.2, 7.4.2.1	Review of laboratory evaluation of suspected hemolytic reactions	5
31	7.4.2.3	Interpretation of the evaluation of suspected immediate transfusion adverse event(s)	5
32	7.4.3	Evaluation and interpretation of delayed transfusion adverse event(s)	5
33	7.4.6	Look-back to identify recipients who may have been infected with HCV or HIV viruses	10

[1]Applicable state or local law may exceed this period.
[2]21 CFR 606.160(d).

Reference Standard 6.2C–Retention of Other Documents and Records

Item No.	Standard	Record to Be Maintained	Minimum Retention Time (in years)[1,2]
1	1.2.2	Management review of effectiveness of the quality system	5
2	1.3.2	Exceptions to policies, processes, and procedures	5
3	2.1	Job descriptions	5
4	2.1.1	Qualification of personnel performing critical tasks	5
5	2.1.2	Training records of personnel	5
6	2.1.3	Evaluations of competence of personnel	5
7	2.1.4	Personnel records of each employee	5
8	2.1.4.1	Records of names, signatures, initials, or identification codes, and inclusive dates of employment for personnel who perform or review critical tasks	10
9	3.2	Equipment qualification	5
10	3.3	Equipment validation	5
11	3.4	Unique identification of equipment	5
12	3.5	Monitoring and maintenance of equipment	5
13	3.6.2	Temperature monitoring of refrigerators, freezers, and platelet incubators	5
14	3.6.3	Monitoring of liquid nitrogen levels or temperature	5
15	3.9	Implementation and modification of software, hardware, or databases	2 years after retirement of the system
16	3.9.1	1) Validation of system software, hardware, databases, and user-defined tables, electronic data transfer, and/or electronic data receipt 2) Fulfillment of applicable life-cycle requirements	2 years after retirement of the system

Reference Standard 6.2C—Retention of Other Documents and Records (Continued)

Item No.	Standard	Record to Be Maintained	Minimum Retention Time (in years)[1,2]
16 (cont)		3) Numerical designation of system versions, if applicable, with inclusive dates of use 4) Monitoring of data integrity for critical data elements	
17	4.1	Evaluation and participation in selection of suppliers	5
18	4.2	Agreements	5
19	4.2.1	Agreement review	5
20	4.2.2	Agreements concerning activities involving more than one institution	5
21	4.3	Inspection of incoming critical materials and containers	5
22	4.3.2.1	Incoming container, solutions, and reagents meet or exceed applicable FDA criteria	5
23	5.1.1	Validation of new or changed processes and procedures	5
24	5.1.2	Participation in proficiency testing program	5
25	5.1.3	Review of quality control results for reagents, equipment, and methods	5
26	5.1.4.1	Reagents prepared by facility meet or exceed FDA criteria	5
27	5.1.8.2.1	Ambient temperature recorded every 4 hours when components are stored in open storage area	5
28	5.1.8.2	Inspection before shipping	5
29	5.19.1	Participation in development of policies, processes, and procedures regarding recipient consent for transfusion	5

(Continued)

Reference Standard 6.2C—Retention of Other Documents and Records (Continued)

Item No.	Standard	Record to Be Maintained	Minimum Retention Time (in years)[1,2]
30	6.1.3	Review and approval of new and revised documents before use	5
31	6.1.4	Annual review of policies, processes, and procedures	5
32	6.1.6	Identification and appropriate archival of obsolete documents	5
33	7.0, 7.1	Description and evaluation of nonconforming blood, components, tissue, derivatives, critical materials, and services	5
34	7.1.4	Nature of nonconformances discovered after release and subsequent actions taken, including acceptance for use	5
35	7.4.5.1	Transfusion service reporting of transfusion-transmitted diseases	10
36	8.1.2	Review of assessment results	5
37	8.2	Peer-review assessment of blood utilization	5
38	9.0	Implementation of changes to policies, processes, and procedures resulting from corrective and preventive action	5
39	9.1	Corrective action	5
40	9.2	Preventive action	5
41	10.2	Monitoring of biological, chemical, and radiation safety	5
42	10.3	Appropriate discard of blood and components	10

[1]Applicable state or local law may exceed this period.
[2]21 CFR 606.160(d).

Reference Standard 6.2D—Retention of Tissue Records

Item No.	Standard	Record to Be Maintained	Minimum Retention Time (in years)[1,]
1	4.3	Inspection of incoming tissue upon receipt	10
2	5.11.1	Requests for tissue	10
3	5.15.3	Preparation and dispensing of tissue	10
4	5.18.2.1	1) Identification number or other product identifier provided by the manufacturer 2) Product expiration date 3) The manufacturer's package insert documents are present and are issued 4) The date and time of issue	10
5	5.19.6.1	Identity of source facility, identification of ordering personnel, name and address of consignee, type of tissue, numeric or alphanumeric identifier, quantity, collection and/or expiration date, personnel who prepare the tissue for dispensing, personnel who dispense the tissue, date of dispensing, date of use and, if tissue is not transplanted, final tissue disposition	10 years beyond the date of final disposition
6	7.1	Identification of nonconforming tissue	10
7	7.4.4	Investigation of adverse effects, disease transmission, or other suspected adverse event(s) of tissue use and reporting such cases to the source facility and outside agencies as required	10
8	10.3	Appropriate discard of tissue	10

[1]Applicable state or local law may exceed this period.

Reference Standard 6.2E—Retention of Derivative Records

Item No.	Standard	Record to Be Maintained	Minimum Retention Time (in years)[1]
1	4.3	Inspection of incoming derivatives upon receipt	10
2	5.11.1	Requests for derivatives	10
3	5.15.4	Preparation or dispensing of derivatives	10
4	5.18.2.1	1) Identification number or other product identifier provided by the manufacturer 2) Product expiration date 3) The manufacturer's package insert documents are present and are issued 4) The date and time of issue	10
5	5.19.6.2	Identity of supplier, identification of ordering physician or other authorized health professional, type of derivative, lot number, quantity, collection and/or expiration date, personnel who prepare and dispense the derivative, date of dispense, final inspection before dispense, personnel who accept the derivative for use, identifying information (two independent identifiers) about intended recipient, if available, date of infusion, and, if not infused, final derivative disposition	10 years beyond the date of distribution, date of infusion, date of disposition, or date of expiration, whichever is the latest date
6	7.1	Identification of nonconforming derivatives	10
7	7.4.4	Investigation of adverse effects, disease transmission, or other suspected adverse event(s) of derivative use and reporting such cases to the source facility and outside agencies as required	10
8	10.3	Appropriate discard of derivatives	10

[1]Applicable state or local law may exceed this period.

7. DEVIATIONS, NONCONFORMANCES, AND ADVERSE EVENTS

7.0 Deviations, Nonconformances, and Adverse Events

The blood bank or transfusion service shall have policies, processes, and procedures to ensure the capture, assessment, investigation, and monitoring of deviations from meeting, or failing to meet, specified requirements. The responsibility for review and authority for the disposition of nonconforming blood, components, tissue, derivatives, critical materials, and services shall be defined. Deviations, nonconformances, and adverse events shall be reported in accordance with specified requirements and to outside agencies as required.[*]

7.1 Nonconformances

Upon discovery, nonconforming blood, components, tissue, derivatives, critical materials, and services shall be evaluated and their disposition determined.

7.1.1 Nonconforming blood, components, tissue, and derivatives shall be quarantined.

7.1.2 Blood, components, tissue, derivatives, critical materials, or services that do not conform to specified requirements shall be prevented from unintended distribution or use.

7.1.3 The blood bank or transfusion service shall have a process for:
1) The identification, quarantine, retrieval, and recall of nonconforming blood, components, tissue, and derivatives.
2) The identification and management of nonconforming services.
3) Notification of users, suppliers, and outside agencies as required.

7.1.4 Released Nonconforming Blood, Components, Tissue, or Derivatives

Blood, components, tissue, or derivatives that are determined after release not to conform to specified requirements shall be evaluated to determine the effect of the nonconformance on the quality of the product. In cases where quality may have been affected, the nonconformance shall be reported to the customer. Records of the nature of

---

[*]21 CFR 606.171(b).

nonconformances and subsequent actions taken, including acceptance for use, shall be maintained. Standard 9.1 applies.

7.2 Fatality Reporting
Fatalities related to blood donation or blood transfusion shall be reported to outside agencies as required.*

7.3 Adverse Events Related to Donation
Adverse events related to the blood donation process shall be assessed, investigated, and monitored.

7.4 Adverse Events Related to Transfusion
There shall be a process for the administration of blood and components that includes the recognition, evaluation, and reporting of suspected transfusion-related adverse events. The medical director shall participate in the development of protocols used by the transfusing staff to identify, evaluate, and report adverse events related to transfusion. Standards 1.1.1 and 5.19 apply.

7.4.1 Recognition of and Response to Immediate Transfusion Reactions
There shall be processes and procedures for the transfusing staff for the recognition of and response to immediate transfusion reactions and for the recording of relevant information in the patient's medical record.

7.4.1.1 The process shall include:
1) Definition of signs and symptoms of suspected transfusion reactions.
2) Indications for interruption or discontinuation of the transfusion.
3) Evaluation and the timely clinical management of the patient.

7.4.1.2 When the transfusion is discontinued the following shall be performed immediately:
1) The label on the blood containers and records shall be examined to detect errors in identifying the patient, blood, or component.
2) The blood bank or transfusion service and responsible physician shall be notified. Signs and symptoms suggestive of mild allergic reactions (eg, urticaria) need not

---

*21 CFR 606.170(b).

be reported to the blood bank or transfusion service.

3) The blood container (whether or not it contains any blood) shall be sent to the blood bank or transfusion service with, whenever possible, the attached transfusion set and intravenous solutions.

4) A posttransfusion sample shall be obtained from the patient and sent to the blood bank or transfusion service.

7.4.2 Laboratory Evaluation and Reporting of Immediate Transfusion Reactions

The blood bank or transfusion service shall have policies, processes, and procedures for the evaluation and reporting of suspected transfusion reactions, including prompt evaluation, review of clerical information by the blood bank or transfusion service, and notification of the blood bank or transfusion service medical director.

7.4.2.1 For suspected hemolytic transfusion reactions the evaluation shall include:

1) The patient's posttransfusion reaction serum or plasma shall be inspected for evidence of hemolysis. Pretransfusion samples shall be used for comparison.

2) A repeat ABO group determination shall be performed on the posttransfusion sample.

3) A direct antiglobulin test shall be performed on the posttransfusion sample. If the result is positive, the most recent pretransfusion sample shall be used for comparison.

4) The blood bank or transfusion service shall have a process for indicating under what circumstances additional testing shall be performed and what that testing shall be.

5) Review and interpretation by the medical director.

7.4.2.2 The blood bank or transfusion service shall have a process for evaluation for suspected nonhemolytic transfusion reactions including, but not limited to, febrile reactions, possible bacterial contamination, and TRALI.

7.4.2.3 Interpretation of the evaluation by the medical director shall be recorded in the patient's medical record and, if suggestive of hemolysis, bacterial contamination, TRALI, or other serious adverse event related to transfusion, the interpretation shall be reported to the patient's physician immediately. Standard 7.4.2.4 applies.

7.4.2.4 When a transfusion fatality or other serious, unexpected adverse event occurs that is suspected to be related to an attribute of a donor or a unit, the collecting facility shall be notified immediately and subsequently in writing.

7.4.3 Delayed Transfusion Reactions (Antigen-Antibody Reactions)

If a delayed transfusion reaction is suspected or detected, tests shall be performed to determine the cause. The results of the evaluation shall be reported to the patient's physician and recorded in the patient's medical record. Standard 7.4.2.4 applies.

7.4.4 Adverse Events Related to Tissue or Derivatives

The blood bank or transfusion service shall have a process for investigating adverse effects, disease transmission, or other suspected adverse events related to the use of tissue and derivatives and for promptly reporting such cases to the source facility and outside agencies as required. Standards 7.4.5 and 7.4.6 apply.

7.4.5 Transfusion-Transmitted Diseases

7.4.5.1 **Transfusion Service Reporting of Transfusion-Transmitted Diseases**

The transfusion service shall have policies, processes, and procedures to evaluate and report transfusion-transmitted diseases. The policies, processes, and procedures shall include the following:

7.4.5.1.1 Prompt investigation of each event by the medical director.

7.4.5.1.2 If transmission is confirmed or not ruled out, the identity of the implicated donor units shall be reported to the collecting facility.

7.4.5.2 **Collection Facility Investigation of Transfusion-Transmitted Diseases**

The collection facility shall have policies, processes, and procedures for investigation of reports of transfusion-transmitted diseases, deferral of donors, and reporting findings to the transfusing facility.

7.4.6 Look-Back

7.4.6.1 Collection Facility
The collection facility shall have policies, processes, and procedures to notify consignees of blood or blood components from donors subsequently found to have, or be at risk for, relevant transfusion-transmitted diseases.*

7.4.6.2 Transfusion Services
The transfusion service shall have policies, processes, and procedures to:

7.4.6.2.1
Identify recipients, if appropriate, of blood or components from donors subsequently found to have, or to be at risk for, relevant transfusion-transmitted infections.

7.4.6.2.2
Notify, if appropriate, the recipient's physician and/or recipient as specified in FDA regulations and recommendations.*

---

*21 CFR 610.46-48 and 42 CFR 482.27(c).
FDA Guidance for Industry, August 24, 2007, "Lookback for Hepatitis C Virus (HCV): Product Quarantine, Consignee Notification, Further Testing, Product Disposition, and Notification of Transfusion Recipients Based on Donor Test Results Indicating Infection with HCV."

8. ASSESSMENTS: INTERNAL AND EXTERNAL

8.0 Assessments: Internal and External

The blood bank or transfusion service shall have policies, processes, and procedures to ensure that internal and external assessments of operations and quality systems are scheduled and conducted.

8.1 Management of Assessment Results

The results of internal and external assessments shall be reviewed by personnel having responsibility for the area being assessed.

8.1.1 When corrective action is taken, it shall be developed, implemented, and evaluated in accordance with Chapter 9, Process Improvement Through Corrective and Preventive Action.

8.1.2 The results of internal and external assessments and associated corrective and preventive actions shall be reviewed by executive management.

8.2 Monitoring of Blood Utilization

Transfusing facilities shall have a peer-review program that monitors and addresses transfusion practices for all categories of blood and components. The following shall be monitored:

1) Ordering practices.
2) Patient identification.
3) Sample collection and labeling.
4) Infectious and noninfectious adverse events.
5) Near-miss events.
6) Usage and discard.
7) Appropriateness of use.
8) Blood administration policies.
9) The ability of services to meet patient needs.
10) Compliance with peer-review recommendations.
Chapter 9, Process Improvement Through Corrective and Preventive Action, applies.

9. PROCESS IMPROVEMENT THROUGH CORRECTIVE AND PREVENTIVE ACTION

9.0 Process Improvement Through Corrective and Preventive Action

The blood bank or transfusion service shall have policies, processes, and procedures for data collection, analysis, and followup of issues requiring corrective and preventive action, including near-miss events.

9.1 Corrective Action

The blood bank or transfusion service shall have a process for corrective action of deviations, nonconformances, and complaints relating to blood, components, tissue, derivatives, critical materials, and services, which includes the following elements:

1) Description of the event.
2) Investigation of the cause.
3) Determination of the corrective action.
4) Evaluation to ensure that corrective action is taken and that it is effective.

9.2 Preventive Action

The blood bank or transfusion service shall have a process for preventive action that includes the following elements:

9.2.1 Review of information including assessment results, proficiency testing results, quality control records, and complaints to detect and analyze potential causes of nonconformances.

9.2.2 Determination of steps needed to respond to potential problems requiring preventive action.

9.2.3 Initiation of preventive action and application of controls to monitor effectiveness.

9.3 Quality Monitoring

The blood bank or transfusion service shall have a process to collect and evaluate quality indicator data on a scheduled basis.

10. FACILITIES AND SAFETY

10.0 Facilities and Safety

The blood bank or transfusion service shall have policies, processes, and procedures to ensure the provision of safe environmental conditions. The facility shall be suitable for the activities performed. Safety programs shall meet local, state, and federal regulations, where applicable. Standard 1.4 applies.

10.1 Safe Environment

The blood bank or transfusion service shall have processes to minimize and respond to environmentally related risks to the health and safety of employees, donors, volunteers, patients, and visitors. Suitable quarters, environment, and equipment shall be available to maintain safe operations.

10.2 Biological, Chemical, and Radiation Safety

The blood bank or transfusion service shall have a process for monitoring adherence to biological, chemical, and radiation safety standards and regulations, where applicable. Standard 2.1.1 applies.

10.3 Discard of Blood, Components, Tissue, and Derivatives

Blood, components, tissue, and derivatives shall be handled and discarded in a manner that minimizes the potential for human exposure to infectious agents.

LIST OF BLOOD COMPONENT DESCRIPTIONS

Key: ISBT 128 Terminology (Codabar Terminology)

Whole Blood and Red Blood Cell Components

WHOLE BLOOD (Whole Blood): Whole Blood is collected in an anticoagulant/preservative solution and is not further processed. This product should not be used as a source of platelets or labile coagulation factors.

RED BLOOD CELLS (Red Blood Cells): Red cells concentrated by the removal of most of the plasma from sedimented or centrifuged whole blood.

FROZEN RED BLOOD CELLS (Red Blood Cells Frozen): Red Blood Cells that have been stored in the frozen state at optimal temperatures in the presence of a cryoprotective agent.

FROZEN REJUVENATED RED BLOOD CELLS (Red Blood Cells Frozen Rejuvenated): Red Blood Cells that have had 2,3-diphosphoglycerate and adenosine triphosphate restored to normal levels or above and then subsequently exposed to a cryoprotective agent and stored at optimal temperatures in a frozen state.

REJUVENATED RED BLOOD CELLS (Red Blood Cells Rejuvenated): Red Blood Cells that have had 2,3-diphosphoglycerate and adenosine triphosphate restored to normal levels or above.

DEGLYCEROLIZED RED BLOOD CELLS (Red Blood Cells Deglycerolized): Red Blood Cells to which glycerol has been added (eg, as a cryoprotective agent) and subsequently removed by washing with successively lower concentrations of sodium chloride (USP).

DEGLYCEROLIZED REJUVENATED RED BLOOD CELLS (Red Blood Cells Rejuvenated Deglycerolized): Red Blood Cells that have had 2,3-diphosphoglycerate and adenosine triphosphate restored to normal levels or above, subjected to a cryoprotective agent and stored frozen at optimal temperatures. The cryoprotective agent is subsequently removed by washing with successively lower concentrations of sodium chloride (USP).

WASHED RED BLOOD CELLS (Red Blood Cells Washed): Red Blood Cells re-maining after washing with a volume of compatible solution using a method known to remove almost all of the plasma. Depending on the method used, the preparation may contain variable quantities of leukocytes and platelets from the original unit.

RED BLOOD CELLS LOW VOLUME (Red Blood Cells Low Volume): When 300 to 404 mL of whole blood is collected into an anticoagulant volume calculated for 450 ± 45 mL or 333 to 449 mL of whole blood is collected into an anticoagulant volume calculated for 500 ± 50 mL of whole blood.

APHERESIS RED BLOOD CELLS (Red Blood Cells Pheresis): Red Blood Cells in anticoagulant or in anticoagulant and storage solution that have been prepared by automated cytapheresis.

Plasma Components

FRESH FROZEN PLASMA (Fresh Frozen Plasma): Plasma separated from the blood of an individual donor and placed at −18 C or colder within 6 to 8 hours of collection from the donor, or within the time frame specified by manufacturer's instructions.

PLASMA FROZEN WITHIN 24 HOURS AFTER PHLEBOTOMY (Plasma Frozen Within 24 Hours AFTER PHLEBOTOMY): Plasma separated from the blood of an individual whole blood donor and placed at −18 C or colder within 24 hours of collection.

LIQUID PLASMA (Liquid Plasma): Plasma separated from the blood of an individual donor and not frozen.

THAWED PLASMA (This does not exist officially in Codabar): Plasma prepared from Fresh Frozen Plasma or Plasma Frozen Within 24 Hours After Phlebotomy, that has been thawed and stored for up to 5 days.

THAWED PLASMA CRYOPRECIPITATE REDUCED (Thawed Plasma Cryoprecipitate Reduced): Thawed Plasma prepared from Plasma Cryoprecipitate Reduced.

RECOVERED PLASMA (Plasma for Manufacture): Plasma for use in manufacturing and prepared from allogeneic donations. Plasma selected for manufacture that has been collected from whole blood or apheresis plasma collected for transfusion that has expired.

CRYOPRECIPITATED AHF (Cryoprecipitated AHF): The cold insoluble portion of plasma processed from Fresh Frozen Plasma.

POOLED CRYOPRECIPITATED AHF (Cryoprecipitated AHF, Pooled): Two or more units of Cryoprecipitated AHF combined into one bag. The total volume will be indicated on the label. To assist in the pooling process, 0.9% sodium chloride (USP) may be added.

PLASMA CRYOPRECIPITATE REDUCED (Plasma Cryoprecipitate Reduced): Fresh Frozen Plasma from which cryoprecipitate has been removed.

Platelet Components

PLATELETS (Platelets): A suspension of platelets in plasma prepared by centrifugation of whole blood.

POOLED PLATELETS (Platelets Pooled): Two or more units of platelets that have been combined into one bag.

POOLED PLATELETS LEUKOCYTES REDUCED (Platelets Pooled Leukocytes Reduced): Platelets Leukocytes Reduced are prepared by a method known to reduce the leukocyte number to $<5 \times 10^6$. A suspension of platelets in plasma that has been leukocyte reduced. The leukocyte reduction process can take place either before or after the pooling process.

APHERESIS PLATELETS (Platelets Pheresis): A suspension of platelets in plasma prepared by cytapheresis. Whole Blood undergoes centrifugation in a cell separator, with the return to the donor of components not collected.

APHERESIS GRANULOCYTES (Granulocytes Pheresis): A suspension of granulocytes in plasma prepared by cytapheresis.

APHERESIS GRANULOCYTES/PLATELETS (Granulocytes/Platelets Pheresis): A suspension of granulocytes in plasma prepared by cytapheresis, with the concurrent collection of platelets.

GLOSSARY

Adverse Event: A complication in a donor or patient. Adverse events may occur in relation to a donation, a transfusion, or a diagnostic or therapeutic procedure.

Agreement: A contract, order, or understanding between two or more parties, such as between a facility and one of its customers.

Agreement Review: Systematic activities carried out before finalizing the agreement to ensure that requirements are adequately defined, free from ambiguity, documented, and achievable.

Assessment: A systematic, independent examination that is performed at defined intervals and at sufficient frequency to determine whether actual activities comply with planned activities, are implemented effectively, and achieve objectives. Assessments usually include comparison of actual results to expected results. Types of assessments include external assessments, internal assessments, quality assessments, peer-review assessments, and self-assessments.

Backup: Digital data storage media (magnetic tape, disc, CD, etc) containing copies of computer data.

Blood Bank: A facility that performs, or is responsible for the performance of, the collection, processing, storage, and distribution of human blood and/or components intended for transfusion and transplantation.

By a Method Known to: Use of published data to demonstrate the acceptability of a process or procedure, particularly for component preparation.

Certified by the Centers for Medicare and Medicaid Services (CMS): Having met the requirements of the Clinical Laboratory Improvement Amendments of 1988 for non-waived testing through inspection by the CMS, a deemed organization, or an exempt state agency.

Change Control: A structured method of revising a policy, process, or procedure, including hardware or software design, transition planning, and revisions to all related documents.

Clinically Significant Antibody: An antibody that is capable of causing shortened cell survival.

Closed System: A system, the contents of which are not exposed to air or outside elements during preparation and separation of components.

Collection Facility: A facility that collects blood, components, or tissue from a donor.

Competence: Ability of an individual to perform a specific task according to procedures.

Compliance: See Conformance.

Components: See List of Blood Component Descriptions.

Conformance: Fulfillment of requirements. Requirements may be de-fined by customers, practice standards, regulatory agencies, or law.

Corrective Action: An activity performed to eliminate the cause of an existing nonconformance, or other undesirable situation in order to prevent recurrence.

Critical Equipment/Materials/Tasks: A piece of equipment, material, service, or task that can affect the quality of the facility's products or services.

Customer: The receiver of a product or service. A customer may be internal (ie, another department within the same organization) or external (ie, another organization).

Cytapheresis: A collection procedure where Whole Blood is removed and separated into components. One or more of the cellular components may be retained, while the remaining elements are combined and returned to the donor or patient.

Derivatives: Sterile solutions of a specific protein(s) derived from blood or by recombinant technology (eg, albumin, plasma protein fraction, immune globulin, and factor concentrates).

Deviation(s): A departure from policies, processes, procedures, applicable regulations, standards, or specifications.

Disaster: An event (internal, local, or national) that can affect the blood supply or the safety of staff, patients, volunteers, and donors.

Document _(noun)_: Written or electronically generated information and work instructions. Examples of documents include quality manuals, procedures, or forms.

Document _(verb)_: To capture information for use in documents through writing or electronic media.

Equipment: A durable item, instrument, or device used in a process or procedure.

Event: A generic term used to encompass the terms "incident," "error," and "accident."

Executive Management: The highest level personnel within an organization, including employees and independent contractors, who have responsibility for the operations of the organization and who have the authority to establish or change the organization's quality policy. Executive management may be an individual or a group of individuals.

Expiration: The last day or time in which the blood, component, tissue, or derivative is considered suitable for transfusion, transplantation, or infusion.

Facility: A location or operational area within an organization. The part of the organization that is assessed by the AABB and receives AABB accreditation for its specific activities.

Final Inspection: To measure, examine, or test one or more characteristics of a unit of blood, component, tissue, or service and compare results with specified requirements in order to establish whether conformance is achieved before distribution or issue.

Guidelines: Documented recommendations.

Inspect: To measure, examine, or test one or more characteristics of a product or service and compare results with specific requirements.

Irradiated: In regard to components, exposed to x-rays or gamma rays at a dose of 25 Gy (2500 cGy) targeted to the central portion of the irradiation canister or irradiation field to prevent the proliferation of T lymphocytes.

ISBT 128: A standard for the identification, labeling, and information processing of blood, cellular therapy, and tissue products. When linear bar codes are used, Code 128 symbology is utilized.

Issue: To release for clinical use (transfusion or transplantation).

Key Quality Functions: Essential job functions that affect the quality of blood, components, or services provided by the organization.

Label: An inscription affixed to a unit of blood, component, tissue, derivative, or sample for identification.

Labeling: Information that is required or selected to accompany a unit of blood, component, tissue, derivative, or sample, which may include content, identification, description of processes, storage requirements, expiration date, cautionary statements, or indications for use.

Lived with: Resided in the same dwelling, home, or dormitory.

Maintain: To keep in the current state.

Material: A good or supply item used in the manufacturing process. Materials are a type of input product. Reagents are a type of material.

Mitigation: Sustained action taken to reduce or eliminate long-term risk to people and property from hazards and their effects.

Near-Miss Event: An unexpected occurrence that did not adversely affect the outcome, but could have resulted in a serious adverse event.

Neonate: A child less than 4 months of age.

Nonconformance: Failure to meet requirements.

Open System: A system, the contents of which are exposed to air and outside elements during preparation and separation of components.

Organization: An institution, or part thereof, that has its own functions and executive management.

Policy: A documented general principle that guides present and future decisions.

Preventive Action: An action taken to reduce the potential for nonconformances or other undesirable situations.

Procedure: A series of tasks usually performed by one person according to instructions.

Process: A set of related tasks and activities that accomplish a work goal.

Process Control: The efforts to standardize and control processes in order to produce predictable output.

Product: A tangible result of a process or procedure.

Proficiency Testing: The structured evaluation of laboratory methods that assesses the suitability of processes, procedures, equipment, materials, and personnel.

Qualification: With respect to individuals, the aspects of an individual's education, training, and experience that are necessary to successfully meet the requirements of a position. Specifically for equipment, verification that specified attributes required to accomplish the desired task have been met.

Quality: Characteristics of a unit of blood, component, tissue, derivative, sample, critical material, or service that bear on its ability to meet requirements, including those defined during agreement review.

Quality Control: Testing routinely performed on materials and equipment to ensure their proper function.

Quality Indicator Data: Information that may be collected and used to determine whether an organization is meeting its quality objectives as defined by top management in its quality policy. Indicators are measured by data for movement or regression with regard to those quality intentions. The data used for monitoring a quality indicator may consist of single-source data or multiple-source data, as long as it is clear how the data will come together to define the indicator.

Quality System: The organizational structure, responsibilities, policies, processes, procedures, and resources established by executive management to achieve quality.

Quarantine: To isolate nonconforming blood, components, tissue, derivatives, or materials to prevent their distribution or use.

Reagent: A substance used to perform an analytical procedure. A substance used (as in detecting or measuring a component or preparing a product) because of its biological or chemical activity.

Record *(noun)*: Information captured in writing or through electronically generated media that provides objective evidence of activities that have been performed or results that have been achieved, such as test records or audit results. Records do not exist until the activity has been performed and documented.

Record *(verb)*: To capture information for use in records through writing or electronic media.

Reference Standards: Specified requirements defined by the AABB (see Specified Requirements). Reference standards define how or within what parameters an activity shall be performed and are more detailed than quality system requirements.

Regulations: Rules promulgated by federal, state, or local authorities to implement laws enacted by legislative bodies.

Release: Removal of product from quarantine or in-process status for distribution.

Segregate: To separate or isolate products by a method known to clearly identify them and to minimize the possibility of their unintended distribution or use.

Service: An intangible result of a process or procedure.

Sexual Contact: Any of the following activities (whether or not a condom or other protection was used): vaginal sex (contact between penis and vagina); oral sex (mouth or tongue on someone's vagina, penis, or anus); anal sex (contact between penis and anus).

Shall: A term used to indicate a requirement.

Special Transfusion Requirements: Refers to a patient's medical need for a component that has been modified, such as components that are irradiated, washed, or leukocyte reduced; components from special sources, such as autologous or directed; components that need special handling (eg, being subjected to the heat of a blood warming device); or that contain special attributes (eg, CMV-seronegative or antigen-negative).

Specified Requirements: Any requirements in these *BB/TS Standards* including but not limited to FDA requirements; requirements of a facility's internal policies, processes, and procedures; manufacturers' instructions; customer agreements; practice standards; and requirements of accrediting organizations such as the AABB.

Supplier: An entity that provides an input material or service.

Supplier Qualification: An evaluation method designed to ensure that input materials and services (eg, materials, blood components, tissue and derivatives, patient blood samples) obtained from a supplier meet specified requirements.

Tissue: A group of functional cells and/or intercellular matrix intended for implantation, transplantation, or other therapy (eg, cornea, ligaments, bone). Cellular therapy products covered by the AABB's *Standards for Cellular Therapy Product Services* are not included herein.

Traceability: The ability to follow the history of a product or service by means of recorded identification.

Transfusion-Related Acute Lung Injury: A new acute lung injury (ALI) within 6 hours of a completed transfusion.

Transfusion Service: A facility that performs one or more of the following activities: compatibility testing, storage, selection, and issuing of blood and components to intended recipients. Transfusion services do not routinely collect blood or process Whole Blood into components [except Red Blood Cells and Recovered Plasma].

True Positive: A positive result on both the initial test and the confirmatory test. Specifically for bacteria detection, a confirmatory test is a culture-based test performed on a different sample than the blood culture bottle or other sample used for the initial test. For example, a sample source for the confirmatory test could be the original platelet component. A subculture of the initial positive culture is not an adequate sample for this purpose. If initial testing was culture-based, the confirmatory test can use the same method applied to the alternate sample source.

Unit: A container of blood or one of its components in a suitable volume of anticoagulant obtained from a collection of blood from one donor.

Urticaria Reaction: The development of hives, maculopapular rash, or similar allergic manifestation.

User-Defined Tables: Tables containing data used by computer programs to direct their operations. Typically, user-defined tables contain data that are unique to a specific installation and may change from system to system.

Validation: Establishing recorded evidence that provides a high degree of assurance that a specific process will consistently produce an outcome meeting its predetermined specifications and quality attributes.

Verification: Confirmation by examination and provision of objective evidence that specified requirements have been met.

"CROSSWALK" BETWEEN THE
25TH AND 26TH EDITIONS OF *STANDARDS*

The following "crosswalk" traces each standard in the 25th and 26th editions of *Standards for Blood Banks and Transfusion Services*. Each standard in the 26th edition corresponds with its predecessor in the 25th edition. Standards in the 26th edition appearing in bold are new or have been changed. The "crosswalk" is offered as assistance to those who will be updating their facility's procedures to be compliant with the most current edition of Standards. Its use should not take place of a thorough, line-by-line analysis of each standard.

26th	25th	26th	25th
1.0	1.0	**3.6.1**	3.6.1
1.1	1.1	3.6.2	3.6.2
1.1.1	1.1.1	3.6.3	3.6.3
1.2	1.2	**3.7**	3.7
1.2.1	1.2.1	**3.7.1**	3.7.1
1.2.2	1.2.2	3.7.2	3.7.2
1.3	1.3	3.7.3	3.7.3
1.3.1	1.3.1	**3.8**	3.8
1.3.2	1.3.2	3.9	3.9
1.4	1.4	3.9.1	3.9.1
1.5	**New**	3.9.2	3.9.2
2.0	2.0	3.9.3	3.9.3
2.1	2.1	3.9.4	3.9.4
2.1.1	2.1.1	3.9.5	3.9.5
2.1.2	2.1.2	4.0	4.0
2.1.3	2.1.3	4.1	4.1
2.1.4	2.1.4	4.1.1	4.1.1
2.1.4.1	2.1.4.1	4.1.2	4.1.2
3.0	3.0	4.1.2.1	4.1.2.1
3.1	3.1	4.2	4.2
3.2	3.2	4.2.1	4.2.1
3.3	3.3	**4.2.2**	**New**
3.4	3.4	4.3	4.3
3.5	3.5	4.3.1	4.3.1
3.5.1	3.5.1	4.3.2	4.3.2
3.5.1.1	3.5.1.1	4.3.2.1	4.3.2.1
3.5.2	3.5.2	5.0	5.0
3.6	3.6	5.1	5.1

26th	25th	26th	25th
5.1.1	5.1.1	5.3.1	5.3.1
5.1.2	5.1.2	**5.3.2**	5.3.2
5.1.3	5.1.3	5.3.2.1	5.3.2.1
5.1.4	5.1.4	5.3.3	5.3.3
5.1.4.1	5.1.4.1	5.4	5.4
5.1.5	5.1.5	5.4.1	5.4.1
5.1.5.1	5.1.5.1	**5.4.1.1**	5.4.1.1
5.1.5.2	5.1.5.2	**5.4.1.2**	5.4.1.2
5.1.6	5.1.6	5.4.2	5.4.2
5.1.6.1	5.1.6.1	5.4.2.1	5.4.2.1
5.1.6.2	5.1.6.2	5.4.3	5.4.3
5.1.6.3.1 #1	5.1.6.3.1 #1	5.4.4	5.4.4
5.1.6.3.1 #2	5.1.6.3.1 #2	5.4.4.1	5.4.4.1
5.1.6.3.1 #3	5.1.6.3.1 #3	5.4.4.2	5.4.4.2
5.1.6.3.1 #4	5.1.6.3.1 #4	5.4.4.3	5.4.4.3
5.1.6.3.1 #5	5.1.6.3.1 #5	5.4.4.4	5.4.4.4
5.1.6.3.1 #6	5.1.6.3.1 #6	5.4.4.5	5.4.4.5
5.1.6.4	5.1.6.4	5.5	5.5
5.1.6.5	5.1.6.5	5.5.1	5.5.1
5.1.6.5.1	5.1.6.5.1	5.5.2	5.5.2
5.1.6.5.2	5.1.6.5.2	5.5.2.1	5.5.2.1
5.1.6.5.3	5.1.6.5.3	5.5.2.2	5.5.2.2
5.1.7	5.1.7	5.5.2.2.1	5.5.2.2.1
5.1.8		5.5.3	5.5.3
5.1.8.1	5.1.8.1	**5.5.3.1**	5.5.3.1
5.1.8.1.1	5.1.8.1.1	5.5.3.2	5.5.3.2
5.1.8.1.2	5.1.8.1.2	5.5.3.3	5.5.3.3
5.1.8.1.2.1	5.1.8.1.2.1	**5.5.3.4**	**New**
5.1.8.1.3	**New**	**5.5.3.4.1**	5.5.3.4.2
5.1.8.1.4	5.1.8.1.3	**5.5.3.4.2**	5.5.3.4.1
5.1.8.2	5.1.8.2	**5.5.3.4.3**	5.5.3.4
5.1.8.2.1	**New**	5.5.3.5	5.5.3.5
5.2	5.2	5.5.3.5.1	5.5.3.5.1
5.2.1	5.2.1	5.5.3.5.2	5.5.3.5.2
5.2.2	**New**	5.5.4	5.5.4
5.2.3	5.2.2	5.6	5.6
5.2.3.1	5.2.2.1	5.6.1	5.6.1
5.2.3.2	5.2.2.2	**5.6.2**	5.6.2
5.2.4	5.2.3	5.6.2.1	5.6.2.1
5.3	5.3	5.6.3	5.6.3

26th	25th	26th	25th
5.6.3.1	5.6.3.1	**5.7.5.10**	5.7.5.10
5.6.3.1.1	5.6.3.1.1	5.7.5.10.1	5.7.5.10.1
5.6.3.2	5.6.3.2	5.7.5.11	5.7.5.11
5.6.3.3	5.6.3.3	5.7.5.12	5.7.5.12
5.6.4	5.6.4	5.7.5.13	5.7.5.13
5.6.5	5.6.5	5.7.5.14	5.7.5.14
5.6.5.1	5.6.5.1	5.7.5.15	5.7.5.15
5.6.6	5.6.6	**5.7.5.16**	**New**
5.6.6.1	5.6.6.1	5.7.5.17	5.7.5.16
5.6.6.2	5.6.6.2	5.7.5.18	5.7.5.17
5.6.6.2.1	5.6.6.2.1	**5.7.5.19**	5.7.5.18
5.6.7	5.6.7	**5.7.5.20**	5.7.5.19
5.6.7.1 #1	**New**	**5.7.5.21**	5.7.5.20
5.6.7.1 #2	5.6.7.1 #1, 3	5.7.5.22	5.7.5.21
5.7	5.7	5.8	5.8
5.7.1	5.7.1	5.8.1	5.8.1
5.7.2	5.7.2	5.8.2	5.8.2
5.7.2.1	5.7.2.1	5.8.3	5.8.3
5.7.2.1.1	5.7.2.1.1	5.8.3.1	5.8.3.1
5.7.2.1.2	5.7.2.1.2	5.8.3.2	5.8.3.2
5.7.3	5.7.3	5.8.3.3	5.8.3.3
5.7.4	5.7.4	5.8.4	5.8.4
5.7.4.1	5.7.4.1	5.8.4.1	5.8.4.1
5.7.4.2	5.7.4.2	5.8.4.2	5.8.4.2
5.7.4.2.1	5.7.4.2.1	5.8.5	5.8.5, 5.8.5.1
5.7.4.3	5.7.4.3	5.8.5.1	5.8.5.1.1
5.7.5	5.7.5	5.8.6	5.8.6
5.7.5.1	5.7.5.1	5.9	5.9
5.7.5.1.1	5.7.5.1.1	5.9.1	5.9.1
5.7.5.2	5.7.5.2	5.9.2	5.9.2
5.7.5.2.1	5.7.5.2.1	5.9.3	5.9.3
5.7.5.3	5.7.5.3	5.9.4	5.9.4
5.7.5.4	5.7.5.4	5.9.5	5.9.5
5.7.5.5	5.7.5.5	5.9.5.1	5.9.5.1
5.7.5.6	5.7.5.6	5.9.5.2	5.9.5.2
5.7.5.7	5.7.5.7	**5.10**	5.10
5.7.5.8	5.7.5.8	5.11	5.11
5.7.5.8.1	5.7.5.8.1	5.11.1	5.11.1
5.7.5.9	5.7.5.9	5.11.1.1	5.11.1.1
5.7.5.9.1	5.7.5.9.1	**5.11.2**	5.11.2

26th	25th	26th	25th
5.11.2.1	5.11.2.1	5.16.1.2	5.16.1.2
5.11.2.2	5.11.2.2	5.16.1.3	5.16.1.3
5.11.2.3	5.11.2.3	5.16.2	5.16.2
5.11.3	5.11.3	5.16.2.1	5.16.2.1
5.11.4	5.11.4	5.16.2.2	5.16.2.2
5.12	5.12	5.17	5.17
5.12.1	5.12.1	5.17.1	5.17.1
5.13	5.13	5.17.2	5.17.2
5.13.1	5.13.1	5.17.3	5.17.3
5.13.2	5.13.2	5.17.3.1	5.17.3.1
5.13.3	5.13.3	5.17.3.1.1	5.17.3.1.1
5.13.3.1	5.13.3.1	5.17.3.1.2	5.17.3.1.2
5.13.3.2	5.13.3.2	5.17.3.1.3	5.17.3.1.3
5.13.3.3	5.13.3.3	5.17.4	5.17.4
5.13.3.4	5.13.3.4	5.17.5	5.17.5
5.13.4	5.13.4	5.18	5.18
5.13.5	5.13.5	5.18.1	5.18.1
5.13.5.1	5.13.5.1	**5.18.2**	5.18.2
5.13.5.2	5.13.5.2	**5.18.2.1**	**New**
5.14	5.14	5.18.3	5.18.2.1
5.14.1	5.14.1	5.18.4 #1	5.18.3 #1
5.14.2	5.14.2	5.18.4 #2	5.18.3 #2
5.14.2.1	5.14.2.1	5.18.4 #3	5.18.3 #3
5.14.3	5.14.3	**5.18.4 #4**	5.18.3 #4
5.14.4	5.14.4	5.18.5	5.18.4
5.14.5	5.14.5	5.18.5.1	5.18.4.1
5.15	5.15	5.18.5.2	5.18.4.2
5.15.1	5.15.1	5.18.5.3	5.18.4.3
5.15.1.1	5.15.1.1	5.18.5.4	5.18.4.4
5.15.2	5.15.2	5.18.5.5	5.18.4.5
5.15.2.1	5.15.2.1	5.18.5.5.1	5.18.4.5.1
5.15.2.2	5.15.2.2	5.19	5.19
5.15.2.3	5.15.2.3	5.19.1	5.19.1
5.15.2.4	5.15.2.4	5.19.1.1	5.19.1.1
5.15.2.5	5.15.2.5	5.19.2	5.19.2
5.15.3	5.15.3	5.19.3	5.19.3
5.15.4	5.15.4	5.19.4	5.19.4
5.16	5.16	5.19.5	5.19.5
5.16.1	5.16.1	5.19.6	5.19.6
5.16.1.1	5.16.1.1	5.19.6.1	5.19.6.1

26th	25th	26th	25th
5.19.6.2	5.19.6.2	7.1	7.1
5.19.7	5.19.7	7.1.1	7.1.1
5.19.8	5.19.8	7.1.2	7.1.2
5.19.9	5.19.9	7.1.3	7.1.3
5.19.10	5.19.10	7.1.4	7.1.4
5.19.11	5.19.11	7.2	7.2
5.20	5.20	7.3	7.3
5.20.1	5.20.1	7.4	7.4
5.20.2	5.20.2	7.4.1	7.4.1
5.20.3	5.20.3	7.4.1.1	7.4.1.1
5.20.4	5.20.4	7.4.1.2	7.4.1.2
5.20.5	5.20.5	**7.4.2**	7.4.2
5.1.6A	5.1.6A	7.4.2.1	7.4.2.1
5.1.8A	5.1.8A	7.4.2.2	7.4.2.2
5.4.1A	5.4.1A	7.4.2.3	7.4.2.3
6.0	6.0	7.4.2.4	7.4.2.4
6.1	6.1	7.4.3	7.4.3
6.1.1	6.1.1	7.4.4	7.4.4
6.1.2	6.1.2	7.4.5	7.4.5
6.1.3	6.1.3	7.4.5.1	7.4.5.1
6.1.4	6.1.4	7.4.5.1.1	7.4.5.1.1
6.1.5	6.1.5	7.4.5.1.2	7.4.5.1.2
6.1.6	6.1.6	7.4.5.2	7.4.5.2
6.2	6.2	7.4.6	7.4.6
6.2.1	6.2.1	7.4.6.1	7.4.6.1
6.2.1.1	6.2.1.1	7.4.6.2	7.4.6.2
6.2.2	6.2.2	7.4.6.2.1	7.4.6.2.1
6.2.3	6.2.3	7.4.6.2.2	7.4.6.2.2
6.2.4	6.2.4	8.0	8.0
6.2.4.1	6.2.4.1	8.1	8.1
6.2.5	6.2.5	8.1.1	8.1.1
6.2.5.1	6.2.5.1	8.1.2	8.1.2
6.2.5.1.1	6.2.5.1.1	8.2	8.2
6.2.5.1.2	6.2.5.1.2	9.0	9.0
6.2A	6.2A	**9.1 #1**	**New**
6.2B	6.2B	9.1 #2	9.1 #2
6.2C	6.2C	9.1 #3	9.1 #3
6.2D	6.2D	9.2	9.2
6.2E	6.2E	9.2.1	9.2.1
7.0	7.0	9.2.2	9.2.2

26th	25th
9.2.3	9.2.3
9.3	9.3
10.0	10.0
10.1	10.1
10.2	10.2
10.3	10.3

INDEX

Index

Index

Deferrals, donor, 56-61
    autologous, 18
    two-unit red cell apheresis, 20
Deglycerolized Red Blood Cells, 25-26, 48
Deglycerolized Rejuvenated RBCs, 50
Delayed transfusion reactions, 80
Derivatives
    adverse events related to, 80
    corrective action for, 83
    discarding, 84
    expiration of, 55
    handling, 14
    incoming receipt of, 8-9
    inspecting, 8, 14, 32, 38-39
    nonconforming, 77-78
    preparing/dispensing, 36, 39
    quarantine of, 77
    receipt by donors, 57
    records of, 41, 76
    requests for, 32
    storing, 5, 14, 55
    testing, 8
    traceability of, 11, 63
    transporting, 14, 55
Deviations, 77
    corrective action for, 83
    equipment malfunctions, 5
Direct antiglobulin tests, 79
Disaster plans, 2
Discarding products, 84
Documents, 62, 73-74. *See also* Records
Donation intervals
    for apheresis, 18, 19, 20, 56
    for Whole Blood, 19, 56
Donor blood samples
    ABO/Rh testing of, 29, 33
    antibody detection in, 29-30, 35
    collecting, 21-22
    confirmatory testing of, 33
    infectious disease testing of, 15-16, 30-32
    labeling, 21
    retaining, 33
    storing, 22
    weak D in, 29, 33
Donors
    adverse reactions in, 16, 78

blood relatives of recipients, 38
care of, 16
and confidential unit exclusion, 16
consent of, 15-16
dedicated, 45
deferring, 18, 20, 56-61
educating, 15, 16
fatal reactions in, 78
hemochromatosis in, 23
HLA compatible, 38
identification of, 13, 63
implicated in TRALI, 17
notification of abnormal findings in, 16
parental permission for, 15
postdonation information about, 17
postphlebotomy advice for, 16
protection of, 17
qualification of
    allogeneic, 16-17, 56-61
    apheresis, 18-21
    autologous, 17-18
    confidentiality of, 16
records, retention of, 64-67
red cell losses in, 17
safety of, 84
weight of, 18
Drugs
    and donor deferrals, 56-57, 59
    to facilitate leukapheresis, 22
    as transfusion additives, 42

E

Educating donor, 15, 16
Electronic records, 6-7, 63
Emergency preparedness, 2
Employees. *See* Personnel
Environmental safety, 84
Equipment, 4-7
    alarm systems, 5
    calibrating, 4-5
    computer systems, 6-7
    identification of, 4
    malfunctions, failures, or adverse events
        of, 5
    monitoring and maintenance of, 4-5

qualification of, 4
quality control of, 10
selecting, 4
sterility of, 11
storage devices, 5
use of, 4
warming devices, 6
Evaluations
competency, 3
of nonconformances, 77
of transfusion reactions, 79-80
Executive management, 1
Expiration dates and times, 48-55

F

Facilities, 63, 84
Factor VIII, in AHF, 27
Fatalities, 78, 80
Febrile transfusion reactions, 79
Fibrinogen, in AHF, 27
Filters, 42
Forms. *See* Documents
Freezers, 5
Fresh Frozen Plasma, 27, 53-54
Frozen Red Blood Cells, 25, 49, 50

G

Gonorrhea, 59
Graft-vs-host disease, transfusion-associated, 38
Granulocytes
ABO compatibility of, 35
administering, 42
crossmatching, 35
donor intervals for, 19
expiration of, 52
irradiated, 52
preparing, 29
storing, 52
transporting, 52

H

Handling products and materials, 14
Hardware, computer, 6

HBsAg (hepatitis B surface antigen), 30, 31, 58
HCV (hepatitis C virus) RNA, 30, 31, 58
Health, of donors, 57
Hematocrit
of autologous donors, 18
donor requirements for, 56
of Red Blood Cells, 25
of two-unit red cell apheresis, 20
Hemochromatosis, hereditary, 23
Hemoglobin
of Apheresis Red Blood Cells, 20, 26-27
of autologous donors, 18
donor requirements for, 56
Hemoglobin S, 38
Hemolytic transfusion reactions, 79-80
Hepatitis
and donor sexual contacts, 59
history of, in donors, 58
testing for, 30, 31
HIV (human immunodeficiency virus), 30, 31, 58, 59
HLA compatibility, 38
HTLV (human T-cell lymphotropic virus), 30, 31, 58
Human resources, 3

I

Identification. *See also* Labels
of blood samples, 32-33
of components, 13, 38-39
of donors, 13, 63
of equipment, 4
of patients
before blood administration, 41
on blood container label, 38-39
in computer crossmatching, 36
for look-back, 81
monitoring practice of, 82
traceability of, 63
of personnel, 3, 11, 33
Immunizations, 58
Incarceration, of donors, 59
Incubators, platelet, 5
Infants. *See* Neonates
Infectious diseases
component labeling for, 47

Index